MW01519837

Modern woman and how to manage her

Walter M. 1861-1946 Gallichan

Nabu Public Domain Reprints:

You are holding a reproduction of an original work published before 1923 that is in the public domain in the United States of America, and possibly other countries. You may freely copy and distribute this work as no entity (individual or corporate) has a copyright on the body of the work. This book may contain prior copyright references, and library stamps (as most of these works were scanned from library copies). These have been scanned and retained as part of the historical artifact.

This book may have occasional imperfections such as missing or blurred pages, poor pictures, errant marks, etc. that were either part of the original artifact, or were introduced by the scanning process. We believe this work is culturally important, and despite the imperfections, have elected to bring it back into print as part of our continuing commitment to the preservation of printed works worldwide. We appreciate your understanding of the imperfections in the preservation process, and hope you enjoy this valuable book.

Digitized for Microsoft Corporation
by the Internet Archive in 2007.
From University of Toronto.
sed for non-commercial, personal, research,
educational purposes, or any fair use.
not be indexed in a commercial service.

MODERN
WOMAN
AND HOW TO
MANAGE HER

p. 68

SEEN BY
PRESERVATION
SERVICES

DATE................

NEW EDITION.

MODERN MARRIAGE
AND
HOW TO BEAR IT

By MAUD CHURTON BRABY

Crown 8vo, Cloth.   3s. 6d. net.

Part I.—SIGNS OF UNREST. The Mutual Dissatisfaction of the Sexes. Why men don't Marry —Because They Won't. Why Women don't Marry —Because ——? The Tragedy of the Undesired. **Part II.**—CAUSES OF FAILURE. The various Kinds of Marriage. Why we Fall Out; Divers Discords. The Age to Marry. Wild Oats for Wives. A Plea for the Wiser Training of Girls. "Keeping only to Her."—The Crux of Matrimony. **Part III.**—SUGGESTED ALTERNATIVES. Leasehold Marriage à la Meredith. The Fiasco of Free Love. Is legalised Polyandry the Solution? Polygamy at the Polite Dinner Table. A Word for Duogamy. The Advantages of the Preliminary Canter. **Part IV.**—CHILDREN: THE CUL-DE-SAC OF ALL REFORMS. **Part V.**—HOW TO BE HAPPY THOUGH MARRIED. A few Suggestions for Reform. Some Practical Advice to Husbands and Wives. A Word for Love.

MODERN WOMAN
AND
HOW TO MANAGE HER

approx. 1903

By WALTER M. GALLICHAN

Author of

"A SOUL FROM THE PIT"
"THE CONFLICT OF OWEN PRYTHERCH," ETC.

212383
20.5.27

LONDON
T. WERNER LAURIE
CLIFFORD'S INN

CONTENTS

CHAPTER I.

AN AGE LONG CONFLICT.

The Sexes at Variance—In Savage Tribes—Love
and Hate co-existent—Love and the Desire to
Inflict Pain—Why Women Torture their Lovers
—Are Women Gentle?

CHAPTER II.

THE WARFARE TO-DAY.

The Eternal Misunderstanding Between the Sexes—
The Accusation by Women of Men's Selfishness
—Woman as a "Tormenting Joy"—Woman's
Emotionality and its Spurious Outlets—Woman
and Religion—Woman and Art—Nervous
Fatigue in Modern Woman—Why Women
"Nag"—The Tyranny of Woman.

CHAPTER III.

THE DUEL IN LOVE.

Falling in Love—Its Effect upon Men—Its Influence
upon Women—The Differences between the
Love of Men and Women—Engagement—Why
Women like Long Engagements—Why Long
Engagements are often Fatal—Love as a Fine
Art—The Conflict of Lovers—Man-hating
Women, Real and Professed—Militant Spinsters
—Men who fear Women.

CHAPTER IV.

THE WAR IN WEDLOCK.

Ideal Marriage—Marriage as it often is—Why Conjugality is Frequently a State of Warfare—The

CONTENTS

Modern Woman's View of Wedlock—The Profound Ignorance of Husbands—The Profound Ignorance of Wives—The Rift in the Lute—Can it be Mended?—Marriage To-day and in the Future—Is the Free Union a greater success than Marriage?

CHAPTER V.

THE FEUD IN THE FAMILY.

Brothers and Sister—The Clash Between Them—The Quarrels of Parents Concerning the Training of Children—The Revolt of the Daughters—The British Father—The Type Described—The British Matron Described—The Advanced Daughter—The Escape from Home Life—Women in Clubs.

CHAPTER VI.

THE STRIFE OF BREADWINNING.

Women in the Professions and Trades—Their Position—The Rivalry with Men—Is Woman fit to Work?—Moral Effects of Woman's Labour—The " Social Evil."

CHAPTER VII.

THE BATTLE IN POLITICS.

The Dreaded Rule of Women—Intellectual Women—The Struggle for Freedom—The Woman's Suffrage Crusade and its Lessons—Men's Hostility—Portents of the Sex War.

CHAPTER VIII.

CAN THERE BE PEACE?

A Plea for a Freer Association of the Sexes—Feminine Perversity—Sex War as a Cause of Social Dissolution—Supremacy or Equality?—Possibility of Peace.

MODERN WOMAN

AND

HOW TO MANAGE HER

CHAPTER I.

AN AGE-LONG CONFLICT.

THERE has been no period of human history when the sons of men have proved invulnerable to the charms and arts of the daughters of men. The poems of the most primitive singers proclaim the attraction and the grace of Woman, and in all ages poets have acclaimed love with ecstacy and passion. Among the Western nations Woman has been beatified, exalted, even deified. In the East she has stood as the type of ravishing beauty, as the voluptuous charmer of Man, and the reward for his valour or virtue.

Not only among the Eastern races has Woman been regarded as the greatest meed that Man can win. " A crowd of beautiful virgins," it is written in the Edda, " wait the heroes in the Hall of Odin, and fill their cups as fast as they empty them."

In the Age of Chivalry rhapsody upon Woman approached mania. Petrarch and Dante were love-dazed, obsessed by an illusion of Woman. Bernard de Ventadour was willing to relinquish heaven if debarred from seeing his mistress before the throne of God. The Romanticists raved about the beauty, the wit, and the virtue of an ideal being, whom they almost deified, placed on a pedestal, and adored as Woman.

These extravagant eulogies and glowing flatteries might lead us to believe that the adoration of Woman, and the privileges accorded to her, entirely overruled the antagonism of the sexes. There is, however, abundant proof that, in the very height of this craze of Woman Worship, men feared women, personified them as evil, and even hated and despised them.

Renan wittily remarked that the Church raised woman into "the fascination of a sin." While Dante broke into rapture and ecstasy at the purely ideal conception of a maiden, who would probably have thought him a lunatic had he spoken to her, the Church was teaching her children that—

Fierce is the dragon and cunning the asp,
But woman has the malice of both.

Tertullian called woman "the devil's gate";

St. Augustine asked why women were born at all, and warned young men to beware of the Eve in every woman. St. Jerome described woman as "the root of all evil"; and Luther, although he swept away the preposterous doctrine that celibacy is one of the highest moral virtues, advocated the withholding of culture from women on the ground that "no gown worse becomes a woman than the desire to be wise." Under a statute of Henry VIII. "women and others of low condition" were forbidden to read the Scriptures.

I could fill this chapter with quotations from the Fathers, showing how deep was the distrust and the misunderstanding of woman during the period when minstrels and poets sang inflated pæans to the beauty and purity of their mistresses. Many of these pious passages are, to say the least, written in unseemly language; they are all characterised by a spirit of contempt or disgust for women.

Women, in their turn, were either openly or secretly at war with men. The wiser among women discerned the true import of all this adulation. They knew that the angel of to-day was often the demon of to-morrow; and that men ceased to praise them when they set themselves in conflict with male egoism. Many a

queen of chivalry knew that her lord was a poor
fool. Women issued no authoritative and
official denunciation of men, like that of the
ecclesiastic writers concerning women; but then,
as to-day, they talked among themselves of the
stupidity, selfishness, and tyranny of their
spouses, and cultivated the arts of cunning and
strategy, which are ever the weapons of the
enslaved.

The normal antagonism of women towards
men was heightened by the attitude of men.
If a woman exhibited greater intelligence than
the masculine clodpates of her community, she
was exposed to a charge of witchcraft.

Now, the Teutons honoured their " wise
women," who were no doubt the forerunners
of witches; but the wise woman at a later period
was attributed with malign power, and regarded
as a menace to her neighbours. Thousands of
innocent women were tortured during those
Middle Ages that certain writers of *belles lettres*
affect to admire as a romantic golden era. The
proportion of witches vastly outnumbers the
number of wizards who were persecuted.

But what need to speak of the Middle Ages?
Under the Common Law of England, in Boston,
about the year 1850, women were not " persons "
or " citizens," and their husbands could beat

them "with a stick no bigger than his thumb." Women had no personal rights, no ownership in the clothes that they wore, and no claim to the money that they earned. What a glorious era for the domestic Satrap!

The instinctive impulse of woman to tease, torment, and revenge herself upon her owner, Man, was fostered by such means as these. I describe this impulse as fundamental, because it is a phase of love, the strongest passion known to humanity. But it has developed into a systematic warfare, and is now a policy and a method rather than a primitive impulsion.

There are two universal theories concerning women: (1) That she is gentle, and (2) That she is cruel. How have these conflicting views arisen? Why do men when in grief or difficulties so often seek the sympathy and the advice of women? Why, on the other hand, do men declare that women are capable of incredible cruelty? Let us attempt to explain this enigma.

In those countries where marriage by capture still survives, we shall find instructive evidence of that form of the antagonism of the sexes which is inseparable from the great business of love-making. In New Zealand, not long ago, a Maori wooer, with the consent of the girl's

parents, employed force in winning his bride.
He seized the maiden and bore her away,
struggling, biting, kicking. Maori girls are
almost as physically strong as men, and it was
often a wrestling match of fairly equal com-
batants. We read that it was sometimes "the
work of hours" before the captor could carry
the resisting maiden a hundred yards. Thus
love begins among the Maoris, as among other
and more advanced races, with actual cruelty,
strife, and pain.

A Bedouin virgin makes a show of resistance
to her lover by pelting him with stones, which
often wound the suitor. When he grapples
with her, she bites, and uses her fists and nails,
even though she loves him, and desires to be
captured. The European woman does not, as
a rule, display such forms of physical violence;
but the elements of anger, fear, and the desire
to inflict pain enter more or less into most court-
ships.

In Spain, until the middle of the nineteenth
century, women took pleasure in watching a
lover flog himself until the blood flowed; and
the elaborate system of courtship still observed
in that country—which insists that the suitor
should wait for hours, day after day, beneath
the maiden's window till she deigns to smile

upon him—is a survival of the ancient custom of self-torture as a means of winning a woman's favour.

There are cases recorded of women who find exquisite satisfaction in the infliction of both mental and physical pain upon their lovers. Such manifestations are related to the passion of love, and have a very important biological significance.

From this source springs the female instinct of teasing, which is noticeable even among little girls in their play with boys. Every man can recall boyish experiences of this kind. From fourteen up to "sweet seventeen," and sometimes after that age, girls frequently tease, snub, and vex the youths of their acquaintance with much zest. The shyest boys are most exposed to these lacerating snubs. No man dare be as rude as a woman. Her sex protects her from the retaliation of a retort discourteous. This love of tormenting the opposite sex reaches its height in many young girls when a young man is deeply in love with them; and the romantic and ardent types of youths are the chief sufferers from this form of feminine bullying.

Many women relate, in the most cold-blooded terms, stories of their conquests over the affections of men. Their treatment of devoted

suitors is often cruel in the extreme. I have
heard a beautiful woman of this order describe
with gusto the manner in which she first encouraged her lovers, and then, having brought
them to her feet, rejected them with polite
disdain. The spectacle of a man grovelling for
her consent caused acute pleasure.

The emotion that underlies this impulse to
tease men, and to excite their anger, is a phase
of sex-antagonism, but it is very intimately
associated with sexual feeling. The contempt,
the coldness, and the cruelty are unconsciously
directed by the woman towards an end, and they
are frequently the expression of an amative
nature. In its milder forms, unkindness to a
lover is a very common trait among women.
It is often employed to stimulate ardour and to
test a man's devotion. Women who, in love,
first blow hot and then cold by turn are obeying
a primitive instinct, which has played an important part in the relationship of the sexes. When
a woman comes an hour late to the tryst with
her lover, and receives him with coolness,
though on the previous occasion she may have
met him with fervour, she is acting with design
and aforethought. Among animals and savages
this show of indifference is marked, and sometimes highly exaggerated. With civilised

women the tactic is subtle and complex, and often not purely conscious. In the highest types of cultured women, the impulse shrinks almost to the vanishing point. The thoughtful woman, who is as frank about her passions as she is concerning her intellectual opinions, has no use for this artifice, and she condemns it as a device that no longer appeals to the best types of men.

Perfect—that is to say, passionate—love is not without fear on the woman's side. Fear is a stimulant, like pain in certain forms; and there are women who can only love men who are masterful, with a trace of fierceness. Evidence of this fact is to be found in the very numerous instances of women who are strongly attached to harsh and even brutal men. The element of fear, which is a part of modesty, has a physiological use, and nearly all women experience this dread.

When I allude to the cruelty of women, I do not mean that kind of cruelty which men and boys often exhibit in their treatment of animals. There are more men than women among the lovers of sports that inflict pain on brutes. Boys are often fond of annoying and hurting animals, but this tendency is somewhat uncommon among girls. The maternal instinct inhibits this form of cruelty in women; the mother-feeling is protective and pitiful towards the weak and helpless.

Woman's cruelty vents itself upon man, and in some cases upon children. Nothing can excel that callous and malignant cruelty which second wives often display in their treatment of children by a first wife. There are innumerable records of beating, burning, and mutilating children, which might lead us to believe that " the gentle sex " and "a mother's love " are mere poetic figures of speech.

Are women gentle, after all? Yes, they are normally softer, more commiserative and sympathetic, than men; but under stress they are more cruel than our sex. In wars and revolutions women have shown themselves merciless and possessed by a furor of cruelty. It is the women among savage tribes who torture and maim the wounded in battle. And civilised women can commit frightful outrages during revolts and civil wars, when urged to violence by a sense of injury inflicted upon their class or their sex.

A man in an explosion of temper may be cruel and violent, but his cruelty is usually spontaneous and "a short madness," as the ancients said of anger. It is not thoughtfully planned and deliberately carried through. A woman who desires revenge often acts calmly, showing great ingenuity in her methods.

A bruise on the flesh is nothing; a wound upon the sensitive heart is one of the most terrible forms of torture. I do not deny that men often wound women by their speech; but they do not excel, as a sex, in the use of the tongue as a weapon. They are clumsy in retort and invective. Many women are perfect mistresses of mordant sarcasm, and they delight in scarifying their victims. Nagging must be considered presently, but, in passing, we may refer to it as a typical manifestation of feminine cruelty. A scolding wife is a scourge. Better to be flogged periodically with the cat-o'-nine-tails than to be whipped, and stung, and goaded to fury at intervals by a woman's spiteful tongue.

But even a nagging wife may prove a blessing. She is a cure for consumption. In a village where I lived for a few years was a mechanic, disabled for work by lung disease. He was forced to spend the whole day in the company of his wife, who was a terrible termagant. The perpetual nagging and chiding became unbearable. At last the wretched man made it his custom to go out and sit in the fields whenever his wife began to rate him. And to this I attribute his recovery from consumption. It was the rest and open-air remedy. But if his wife's tongue had not driven him out of the house, he could never have adopted this sanitary method. There is no evil without good in it. I have heard of men being " nagged to death." This man was nagged to life.

Whether a gentle woman is more gentle than a gentle man I have never been able to decide. I think that a woman perceives more quickly than a man when she is causing irritation or pain. This accounts perhaps for her frequent superiority both as a healer and as one who wounds. She apprehends quickly that which will soothe or irritate, and acts on either impulse with palpable results. If she wishes to plunge you into hell, she will do it ruthlessly. If she desires to lift you into the seventh heaven, she will raise you by a sweet exercise of her intuition and gentleness. A woman can be more like an angel than a man. She can also prove more like a fiend.

I hear my women readers objecting to this. Women usually assert that men cause more suffering to women than women inflict upon men. How can you tell, dear woman reader? You are not a man; only a man can affirm the amount of pain that a woman causes him. We can only say that the sexes torment one another in a very appalling fashion.   And the appraising of the degree of suffering is a mere matter of experience and comparison.   It cannot be tested by precise calculations, nor by means of an instrument.   Therefore, it must remain an open and debatable point.

CHAPTER II.

THE WARFARE TO-DAY.

"MEN don't understand us." How many times, my man reader, have you heard this statement in the course of your life? I have heard it reiterated times without number, and I shall continue to hear it until I die.

"Men don't understand us." I can visualise at least a score of women, of different ages and of varying degrees of charm, uttering this formula in diverse tones, from the tenderly pathetic to the fiercely combative.

No, we do not understand woman, nor does she understand us, wholly and rightly. Men undoubtedly understand women more than women would care to admit, but the comprehension is incomplete on both sides. How can man understand woman when she admittedly cannot understand herself?

I propose to bring up the chief indictments of women against my sex, and to weigh the testimony as judicially as I am able. I will then sift the evidence of men against women. The foremost accusation directed at men by women is that they are Selfish. I give the adjective a capital letter to emphasise it; for we all know how emphatically women pronounce this word when we stand shivering in the domestic tribunal, trying to explain and to excuse ourselves.

"Men *are* so selfish"; the stress, if you will notice, is generally laid upon the "are." I have heard this charge so often that I have almost begun to doubt its veracity. That everyone is selfish is a good generalisation to work upon; that the male human being is more selfish than woman is a rather different postulate.

What is selfishness? My dictionary definition is: " The exclusive regard of a person to his own interest or happiness; or that supreme self-love or self-preference which leads a person in his actions to direct his purposes to the advancement of his own interest, power, or happiness, without regarding the interest of others. Selfishness, in its worst or unqualified sense, is the very essence of human depravity, and stands in direct opposition to benevolence, which is the very essence of the divine character. As God is love, so man, in his natural state, is selfishness. Selfishness: a vice utterly at variance with the happiness of him who harbours

it, and as such condemned by self-love."—
Mackintosh.

Let us take breath. If "man in his natural
state is selfishness," we must all, men and
women, alike plead guilty. We are all un-
righteous; we are all fools, and we are all selfish.
What concerns us for the moment is whether
women are right in burdening men with so
heavy a share in this guilt of self-love.

I see in one of the groves or avenues of
Tooting a middle-aged citizen of the male sex,
eternally panting to catch the 9.14, which takes
him each day to Basinghall Street. I see him
through an æon, seated at a desk in a stuffy
office, surrounded by the driest of tomes that
go by the name of books, writing, calculating,
and endeavouring to do that duty to which Fate
has called him. Once a year he goes to the
seaside for a fortnight, trifles with a golf club,
takes his morning plunge in the sea, and
tries to forget what a terrible machine he is when
in Basinghall Street for the rest of the year.
The few green spots in the desert of his life
could be counted on his fingers.

In the scheme of things what is he? The
eternal protector of the brood, the house-band,
the guid man, the paterfamilias, the English
papa. Once he stalked almost nude in the

woods, with a stone axe in his hand, looking for a rival hunter to brain, or a beast of venery to slay. He was more picturesque in those day, common one. And yet we know well his weapons are in the British Museum, and a cheap frock-coat and trousers hide the natural man. You may say that he is just doing his simple duty. Quite so; but he would much prefer to play golf, or to potter about his garden, and might do so were it not for the desire to make his children's lives easier than his life was in childhood. Instead of retiring at fifty-five, which he could do if he stinted his wife and daughters in their dress allowance, he will continue to drudge in the City until he is senile and worn-out.

Now, this worthy person is typical; I have not selected an unusual instance, but an every-day common one. And yet we know well enough that he will not escape the reproach of his women-folk that he is selfish. Of course he is selfish. Is he not a man? This pampered epicure drinks a bottle of wine occasionally and smokes fourpenny cigars. He is also guilty of travelling second-class instead of third-class. Is he not proved guilty? Assuredly he is a selfish man. He always occupies the most comfortable easy chair when he comes home tired from the

City.   What need have we to add to the list of his offences?   He is a selfish man.

Modern women assure us that, through the selfishness of men, they are unable to live their own lives.   The man who pays the piper calls the tune, and women have to dance to it.   In the blissful millennium of " the economic freedom of women," which I, for one man, hope to realise, women will change all this.   What living one's own life means precisely I have never discovered.   No man can live his own life, if he is poor or married.   No woman can live her own life, if she wishes to set men an example of unselfishness.

Let us take a few common instances of the alleged inordinate selfishness of men.   Edwin and Angelina have been married a year, and the question of the annual holiday is discussed by them.   " My dear," remarks Edwin, "I would like to go to Bournemouth for our holidays. There are good golf links there."

Angelina looks solemn.   She is silent while Edwin dilates on the joys of Bournemouth. Presently she speaks; her forehead is ruffled, and her voice is curious, distant, and polite, like that of a stranger.   Selfish Edwin is astonished.

" What, you don't want to go to Bourne-mouth ? "

" You know I wanted to go to Hastings."

" But I hate Hastings."

" Has it never struck you that I may hate Bournemouth? As a matter of fact, I have often said that Bournemouth is detestable."

Edwin is glum for several moments.

" Well, my dear," he resumes, I'll go to Hastings if *you* like, but you know I shan't enjoy it."

" Oh, if you won't enjoy it, for goodness' sake don't go.   I don't want to drag you to Hastings against your will. . . . I'll go to Bournemouth. It is always the woman who has to give in."

Angelina emits a deep, hollow sigh, and folds her hands resignedly upon her lap, looking the very picture of martyrdom.   Edwin mutters, takes up the newspaper, and goes away to sulk.

Yes, I suppose Edwin, in this case, is abominably selfish.   But how do you describe Angelina's conduct?   Her mere asseveration that it is "always the woman who has to give in" proves that she is both inaccurate and selfish. Edwin—unless we must believe him to be an utter brute—very often "gives in" to Angelina. But she does not choose to remember this.   It would be treachery to her principles to remember it. Deeply dinted into her brain is the impression that men are selfish, and that women always give in to them in the long-run. She must be faithful to this feminine creed.

"There is more quarrelling in married life about whether a window shall be open or shut than from any other cause," said a woman to me. I think it *is* the minor issues that cause the most friction between average married folk. The conflict of egoisms is not so often urged upon great causes as upon comparative trifles. And, unless both the man and his wife are capable of constant compromise, we witness scenes of domestic discord and fury. To "give in" gracefully and with dignity is not an easy art in any form of partnership. It is, however, a most necessary accomplishment.

Another accusation levelled by women against men is that of coarseness and sensuality. I do not deny that a large number of men are coarse in thought and speech. Most men are plainer and ruder than women in their conversation. But if coarseness is the masculine note, vulgarity is the prevailing feminine note, in allusion to certain vital subjects. Men jest indecently about the physical relationship of the sexes, and in all classes of society, sex is a topic of flippant, unseemly, and extremely stupid conversation. Women, as a rule, are not coarse-minded; they do not engage in obscene jokes about the corporeal aspect of the love-passion, but many women talk of love with a mixture of cynicism and vulgarity that is akin to grossness.

The coarseness of men and the flippant vulgarity of women in the discussion of love are phenomena of so-called civilised communities, wherein decent frankness in sex matters is inhibited by prudery. In those countries where religion is harsh, and the priest in the ascendant, blasphemy is a common offence. Men deride sacred things, and take the name of the holy in vain, whenever religion is oppressive and a menace to the enjoyment of worldly pleasures. Mystery and taboo surround religions, and the same mystery and prohibitory restrictions upon open discussion surround the deeply important subject of sex.

Human perversity finds a relief and pleasure in jesting upon those topics, which society has set aside as unmentionable except in furtive whispers. Hence coarseness in men, and levity in women, in the everyday allusion to love between the sexes, is a reaction against an unnatural and injurious reticence. Impurity of thought is common in both sexes. It is only its expression that differs. I can point to many men and women who are pure in body, but I have met very few who are pure in thought.

In regard to sex we are in a most unwhole-
some and diseased state of mind, and until our
minds are purged from the twin evils of prudery
and coarseness, moral reform is impossible in
that great field of thought and action controlled
by the sex-impulse. We need to substitute
clean plain-speaking for the sly whisper, the
foolish veiled allusion, the unclean joke, and
the indecent snigger.

The sensuality of men is a frequent reproach.
Here, again, it is only a question of difference
between the sexes in the manifestation of pleasure in the indulgence of the senses. In a
highly complex state of civilisation sensuality
is increased by constant stimulation and a
heightened imagination. There is a false view,
often advanced by preachers and writers, that
savages are exceedingly lascivious and grossly
sensual. Savages, living under healthy primitive conditions, are continent, and even ascetic,
in comparison with cultured races living in ease
and luxury. The amative passions of the refined
man or woman are very frequently in a state
of hyperæsthesia through a hundred stimulating
influences.

The love of women for dainty food, soft beds,
luxurious and well-warmed rooms, pretty
dresses, and personal ornaments is sensual.

Jeremy Taylor gave thanks to God for his
sensual pleasures, and if we are healthy-minded
we shall do the same. There is no cause for
shame in the satisfaction which we derive from
a well-prepared and relishing dinner, a glass of
wine, or a cigar. If we believe in a beneficent
Creator, we insult His wisdom by pretending
that the pleasure of the gustatory sense is sinful
or unworthy. If we believe in the intelligence
of Nature, we should surely recognise that our
nervous systems were given us as a means of
recording pleasureable as well as painful sensa-
tions.

Wholesome satisfaction of the desires of the
senses is so commonly confused with disordered
desires that we prate about "sensual pleasure"
as something abnormal or evil. Women are
more prone than men to talk this kind of cant.
In a large measure, the teaching of the
Catholic Church is the source of this unnatural
recoil against perfectly harmless, and indeed
beneficial, enjoyment of the senses. The pro-
scriptions and penalties have defeated their ends;
and in the reaction men have become more and
not less sensual, through the fanatical teaching
of absolute chastity as a high virtue.

In *The English Woman*, an instructive book
by David Staars, a Frenchman, the author says

that women look upon men as big children. I
have often heard this comparison of men with
children uttered by the Modern Woman. In
a very healthy and admirable manner men *are*
children. They retain the freshness, keenness,
and simplicity of childhood longer than women.
They have more hobbies than women; they play
oftener and more naturally, and they are less
concerned to appear on their dignity.

A woman soon ceases to be youthful because
she is so conscious of the fact that she is a
woman, and so palpably anxious to avoid appear-
ing skittish or ridiculous. I have noted this
difference between the sexes when directing a
company of village players. The men and boys
threw themselves into a comic part with a simple
regard for acting. The women and girls were
afraid that they might appear ridiculous in the
eyes of their friends, and they were three times
as self-conscious as the men players. They had
no wish to be funny; they wanted to look pretty
and, at the same time, dignified. The explana-
tion is that woman is condemned to pose; she
cannot permit herself to be childish, and she dare
not romp after eighteen at the latest.

In a man's club known to me, I often see
portly members of fifty or sixty romping like
schoolboys, and the spectacle delights me. It

is a splendid thing to retain some of the high
spirits of boyhood.   Remember, too, that the
genius is akin to the child.   You do not insult
a man by calling him a " great boy."   It is not
a mark of a feeble intelligence to take pleasure
in simple things.   It is often the sign of a great
mind, and this may be easily proved by collecting
a few facts upon the recreations of learned and
illustrious men.

When we consider that most of the big affairs
of life are in the hands of men, and that the
world has jogged along fairly well, we need not
feel affronted when women declare that we are
" only children."

In their own feminine way, women are as
childlike as men.   Their talk is generally sillier
than ours; they are full of puerile conceits, and
they are, in their own manner, quite as frivolous
as their brothers.   Go into the main streets of
the West End of London upon any afternoon,
and you will see crowds of women of every age
blocking the traffic on the pavements, while they
gaze at the useless whim-whams and bits of
ribbon in the shop windows.   Yet if a man goes
fishing, or plays games, these women will smile
pityingly, and call him " a big child."

Irascibility is another specific failing ascribed
by women to men.   But men have not the

monopoly of this characteristic; and I seriously
doubt whether they are, on the whole, as irritable
and prone to outbursts of ill-temper as women.
Breakings-out in our asylums are commoner in
the female than the male wards. I can see very
little difference between the bluster of a choleric
man and the anger of a nerve-tired, hysterical
woman. In both cases we have an explosion,
and generally the explosion is more prolonged
in the case of the woman, though it may be less
violent.

This brings us to the consideration of
feminine nagging, its cause and nature. The
widespread prevalence of scolding among
women has given rise to many cynical aphorisms
upon a woman's tongue and the sting in it.
Our ancestors invented the brank, or scold's
bridle, an instrument of penance worn by contentious wives as a cure for nagging.

Nagging is a form of feminine energy.
Woman's tongue is fluent and glib, and she is
fond of employing that organ. Often she scolds
automatically, as it were, as a thrush sings in a
wet dawn. Most women tend to scold unduly.
The working woman uses the most dire and
terrible threats towards her children, without
any intention of carrying them into practice.
It relieves her feelings to nag at someone, just

as a sharp storm of temper and "a good swear" relieves the irritated man.

Unfortunately women prolong their scoldings. They go on and on in a lively torrent of words, gaining fresh energy as they proceed. Nagging women are not infrequently murdered by their husbands; they are very often beaten.

There are naggers in all classes. In polite society, a nagging woman is as incisively insolent as her sister of the slums, though her phrases are more refined. The cold, educated nagger is the worst of all. The hysterical woman, sooner or later, weeps and collapses, or becomes a temporary lunatic, and resorts to physical means of displaying her indignation.

Nagging is not wholly a vice. It is a phase of the maternal instinct of reproof and discipline. The impulse to nag must be regarded as common and normal in women, and it is only when the nagging is incessant and excessive that it degenerates into a morbid vice. The best way to manage a nagging woman is to agree with her that you are a perfect brute and wretch; and then to laugh at her. If that fails, fly from her presence.

Woman is more emotional than man. This is shown in many ways; but nothing proves it better than the attitude of women towards

religion, and their taste in the drama and fiction.
Women are said to be more pious than men.
They are certainly more attracted and influenced
than men by the emotional element, the rituals
and the ceremonies of religions.   On the other
hand, the founders of creeds are, among women,
a very insignificant proportion as compared with
the founders of new faiths among men.

Women are the strongest supporters of the
clerical system, and the best friends to the priest.
Students of ecclesiastical history are in a position
to state whether the clergy have been the best
friends of women.   From St. Paul downwards,
the teaching of the Church has not tended to
uplift the status of women, and in many directions that teaching has very seriously hindered
the ideal of sex-equality and a sane association
of the sexes.

Women are not attracted by the more rational
and ethical forms of religion.   They desire
" emotion " in their worship, and this emotion
is very closely allied to the sentiment of love.
Women cheated of the chance of love turn
naturally to religion as a solace and an outlet.
The autobiography of Sœur Jeanne des Anges,
of Loudun, is a human document that casts a
strong light upon the association of religious
mysticism and the emotion of love.

In art it is highly essential that the appeal shall be made to women. Woman is largely responsible for poor and meretricious work in painting, the drama, poetry, and novels. The trail of a forced sentimentality is over our art, and we are gravely afraid of the expression of real, stirring, and vital emotions. This is perhaps more evident in the case of the English novel—which is written chiefly for the amusement of women—than in other " works of art," so-called.

The " lord of creation," man, disports himself in a sort of Fool's Paradise. He imagines that woman is his subordinate. In one sense he is not deluded; but in another sense he is a foolish dupe. The tyranny of woman is tremendous. Man can boast of superior physical strength, a wider range of opportunity, and a more fair and open field of labour than fall to the lot of women. To say this is to state all, and it is not so great and so advantageous to the man as it appears.

The supremest object of Nature is the continuance of the species. Unconscious of the tyranny of woman, man toils all his life in obedience to Nature's behest, and to one main end : to protect the mother and her offspring. From Nature's point of view this is essentially the whole duty of man.

Men think that they are chosen as husbands for their handsome features, their mental qualities, or their charm of disposition. This belief is as vain as it is widespread. Most women select their lover with careful deliberation, and proper regard to his capacity as the faithful breadwinner and the protector. Only a few women are dominated in their choice of a husband by fervid and romantic passion, the emotion that almost deprives many men of reason. Under an economic system that hinders women from earning their own livings, or at the best gives only the scantiest wage, how can we expect the majority of women to take any view of marriage but the arithmetical or the businesslike? Custom and conventional morality deny to women the happiness of love and the joy of motherhood, unless they can secure men who will maintain them and their children in comfort.

Man is the instrument of woman; he is shaped and used for her ends, and in the interest of the species. He imagines that he is the wooer, the captor, and the predominant partner after marriage. Very few men realise the autocracy under which they are doomed to live. Their lordship is a delusion and a sham dignity. They are only the obedient accomplices of women, acting unconsciously in a conspiracy designed by crafty Dame Nature.

CHAPTER III.

THE DUEL IN LOVE.

NATURE takes care that most men and women shall fall in love; and all normal human beings, from the age of sixteen to fifty, and sometimes after that age, are susceptible to the profound emotion of sex-love. Everyone should fall in love at least once in his or her lifetime, for those who have not known love are, in the moral, emotional, and intellectual experiences, lamentably incomplete. I distrust persons who say that they have never been swayed by this passion; and I like them least of all when they vaunt the fact as a sign of superiority or of wisdom.

Why do you ask me to admire you because you are a fish, with fish emotions, a defective nervous and circulatory system, and a lack of imagination?

These fish-men and fish-women are to be pitied. Leave them to the real or pretended enjoyment of their cold-blooded superiority, and do not take them too seriously. They go about the world prating their fish-like warnings and counsels to the warm of blood; while they affect to sneer at those fine emotions that they cannot feel, and tell you that sentiment is absurd. I cannot say to what purpose these fish-persons have been evolved, but I suppose they play some part or another in the economy and scheme of Nature. Nevertheless, if you love woman, as you should do, and have a feeling for .poetry and a soul for romance, avoid the fish-men and fish-women.

The greatest teacher is Love. I defy all the sciences, arts, and philosophies to compete with it. Bernard Shaw may tell his young Fabians that "love is a mawkish sentiment." But, never mind; wiser men than Shaw have realised that this same sentiment is the greatest thing in life. Fortunately, nearly all the world loves the lover, and therein the world is wise. It is easy enough to compose cynical aphorisms about Love, or Socialism, or Religion, or any of the massive passions and ideals. It is not so easy to understand the force, import, and influence of these things. And to some unhappy men, calling themselves artists and thinkers, appreciation of love is denied. Their blood is as water.

A young man in love is an almost awful

spectacle. I can see nothing to laugh at in the serious form of monomania that possesses him. Only fools, blasphemers, and libertines laugh at love. A young man in love may be the most deluded of mortals; but for love's sake let us not shatter his ideal with our mirth or our cynicisms, for an eternal voice speaks within him, and the finest and the noblest aspirations of which he is capable are becoming manifest.

I am struck with the purity of a very large number of youths. An ardent and romantic young man in love is exalted and beatified. His conception of love is even purer than that of a maiden. He would not soil the purity of his love with a single carnal thought. He is the greatest idealist under the sun. To him the maiden is more than queen; he ascribes to her a hundred graces and virtues; and his heart is full of worship. In her presence he trembles and is fearful with adoration. His tongue is tied, and there is vehement agitation in his breast.

Alas! that he should so often fall in love with a shallow-minded, prosaic, hard type of maiden, who cannot possibly share his romantic passion. Is it not because "sweet seventeen" is frequently the least romantic age, that young men

become passionately enamoured of women who
are no longer young?

A boy often conceives a violent affection for
a middle-aged married woman. He finds in her
those qualities for which he yearns, charms of
kindness, sensibility, and softness which are lack-
ing in the young girls of his acquaintance. Love
in a young man is more impetuous and volcanic
than in a young woman. Many other matters
besides the attractiveness or the ardour of her
suitor enter into the thoughts of the average
English girl. She has been schooled to keep
her head; she must love with discretion and due
heed to other things besides romantic fervour.

The middle-aged women who charm boys
know how to love. They have been educated
in the passion, and they are therefore in sympathy with lovers. A young woman, without
experience, is apt to look upon a deeply
enamoured young man as a lunatic. She is
tempted to make fun of him. I know a pathetic
case in which a young shop-boy was " over head
and ears in love," as the saying is, with a girl
of about his own age. Anxious to appear as
gallant and gay as a lover should, he took
especial pains with his ablutions and his clothes
whenever he went to " walk out " with his
sweetheart. One day, in a gush of ardour, he

confessed to the girl that he always "put on his best trousers" when he came to see her. The girl burst into hearty laughter. For her there was no pathos in this admission; she saw only the ridiculous where she should have recognised the sublime.

How would an older woman have received this confession? I do not think she would have laughed at the ingenuous wretch, and made him smart with dismay and shame. She would have realised that the boy was a genuine lover, eager to please her in everything, solicitous that he might appear externally pleasing in her eyes. A mother-feeling—of which a young girl is devoid in relation to a lover—would have welled within her, and I can see her plant a kiss on that poor lad's well-soaped cheeks.

Women, if you have any respect for purity of heart, do not sneer at the fresh young flower of love that springs from the breast of a poetic young man. Be tender and merciful, even if you are amused or bored. You will learn ere long that love is a rare and precious thing, and you may have cause to sigh at another's coldness or cruelty. It is evil to make light of love and to deride its clumsy sincerity in the young.

The very vehemence with which men love renders them somewhat inartistic as lovers.

With women it is different. Professor William
Thomas has an instructive passage upon
woman's share in love-making in his *Sex and
Society* :

"The means of attraction she employs are so
highly elaborated and her technique is so finished
that she is really more active in courtship than
man. We speak of man as the wooer, but
falling in love is really mediated by the woman.
By dress, behaviour, coquetry, modesty, reserve,
and occasional boldness she gains the attention
of man and infatuates him. He does the courting, but she controls the process."

Here, then, is another instance of man's sub-
servience to woman. Even in love he is not the
chief partner in the game; he is swept along by
a mighty physical and psychic force, and becomes
the prey of the woman. This is what every
woman knows. And the power thus entrusted
to her by Nature is very often used tyrannically.
Love caused the death of many gallant knights
in the days of chivalry, and woman's cruel exercise of her ascendancy in love causes much
suffering, and even death, to-day.

"From Samson and Odysseus down, history
and story recognise the ease and the frequency
with which a woman makes a fool of a man,"
writes Professor Thomas. "The male protec-

tive and sentimental attitude is indeed incompatible with resistance." This is very true. Men endure torments, insults, cruelties, and injustices from women that they would quickly resent in their own sex. Woman continually "exploits" man for her own purposes, and man submits.

Are women, then, incapable of a noble, fervent, and constant affection? No, they are sometimes as romantic and reckless in their love as men. One woman's bosom is composed of adamant; another's is tender, yearning, and pitiful. It is not a fundamental sexual characteristic that inhibits so many women from loving with the intense ardour of an amorous man. Woman's coolness in love, her passivity and placidity, arise often from artificial sources. A man-poet speaks of love as "woman's whole existence," but this is not universally accepted by women, nor taught to them as a primary trait of their natures. On the contrary, the prevailing feminine attitude towards love is shamefaced, apologetic, timorous. It is considered "unmaidenly" for a girl to avow that she is consumed with her love for a man. She is taught to conceal such natural and beautiful impulses, and the whole trend of her education in the home and outside of it is towards making her a finished hypocrite in this relation.   Never-theless, she is reared for marriage as her destiny.

A George Sand or a Laurence Hope may write passionately of love; but such women are rare, not only as artists, but as lovers.   This dis-passionate attitude towards love characterises the work of a large number of women novelists. Either from timidity, or from a lack of expe-rience, they write upon the strongest passion of humanity as though men and women were dis-embodied ghosts, instead of warm flesh and blood.

The frigidity, or " sexual anasthæsia," of a great many women appears to be an inherited quality; but we must always remember that such a state of feeling has been induced and fostered by artificial means for many ages, and is probably not a fundamental and specific feminine charac-teristic.   When we consider that the mothers of the community are deemed " modest " and " womanly " in proportion to their ignorance of their own physical life and their natural desires, it is not difficult to understand how this repul-sion has assumed the guise of an abnormality.

Is it not quite conceivable, if we were reared in the belief that it is wrong to savour our food, and that to enjoy the acts of eating and drinking is gross or disgusting, that the gustatory, salivary, and digestive functions would become disordered?   No man can be healthy who spurns his food.   On what a much higher and more psychical plane is the other appetite in question.   It is hardly comparable with the alimentative impulse, being altogether more massive, and intimately connected with the mental and the spiritual.

I refer to this alleged coldness of women, because it is one of the causes of conjugal unhappiness.   Fire and marble are often attracted one to the other by intellectual and moral qualities; and, with no deep understanding of their own needs, the passionate unite with the passionless.   The result is daily before our eyes. We ascribe every reason but the right one to the infelicity that so frequently accompanies such unfortunate unions.   Not one man or woman in a hundred faces the question boldly and sanely.   The tendency everywhere is to deceive oneself and to deceive others upon this vital matter, among many others.

The more thoughtful of our novelists—those who hold the artistic faith that fiction should be a criticism of life by means of a true presentment of the emotions—now and then select this somewhat common characteristic of women for treatment.   I call to mind Thomas Hardy,

Frank Harris, and H. G. Wells as English novelists who do not burk the subject. In *Tono-Bungay* we have a very living portrait of this type of woman. Marion speaks of certain natural and necessary phases of love as " horrid." She represents a large class of women; a class to be pitied, understood, and educated, and not condemned, for they miss many of the finer emotions through the inculcation of false views, and are hardly responsible for their morbidity.

This is an aspect of the antagonism of the sexes which will be properly studied in the future. I say unhesitatingly that the recoil is the source of more domestic misery than can be reckoned, to say nothing of the vice that it causes. It has been plainly recognised by Forel and other scientific investigators; but the average sociologists and writers on the marriage question either avoid the phenomenon or fail to perceive its manifold bearings.

Whether women love differently from men by nature or through training, the fact cannot be disputed that this difference in love is a prevalent cause of disagreement, and even of downright hostility. This disharmony is more likely to arise after than before marriage; for love-making, in England at any rate, is conducted in such a distant and sedate manner that the

lovers hardly know whether they are courting
or talking about tennis. They do not know
enough of one another to quarrel; their minds
are clogged with illusions, and they are both, so
to speak, on their " best behaviour." Of course,
there are tiffs during the engagement; but these
are usually slight skirmishes, and not to be
compared with the terrible " scenes " that are
only too common in married life, when, one by
one, the illusions have vanished like seed-down
in a gale of wind.

A long betrothal has this advantage—that it
affords time for the lovers to cast aside the pose
of best behaviour, and to reveal themselves as
the very human and frail creatures that they are.

If you are frequently in the company of a
woman during a three or four years' engagement,
the probability is that you will quarrel with her
periodically, make it up, " kiss again with tears,"
and live affectionately for another spell of
dormant egoism. Both you and the woman of
your heart will by these means learn something
at least of one another's foibles and defects of
temperament; and if you are philosophic, you
will resolve to bear and forbear in marriage.
Otherwise, your wooing will have a fatal ter-
mination one of these fine days, and there will
be either that farcical-pathetic return of love-

letters and presents, mutual promises of friendship and respect, and so forth, or a tragic explosion and an avowal of contempt, and possibly hatred.

Most women like long engagements. They seriously profess that courtship is more delightful than marriage, and they fear that they will lose the docile, patient, unselfish lover in the husband. I suppose this is an instinctive feeling; but it suggests a somewhat quaint distrust, and is, in a sense, an imputation on the suitor. Men do not fall out of love in marriage so quickly as is commonly supposed. I know that cynics liken wedlock to the tomb of love; and that sour monitors are prone to advise the maiden that it is well to keep the whip-hand over the cringing supplicant for as long as possible; but these grim persons are not wholly reliable as authorities upon marriage.

Prolonged engagements are almost always a mistake. It is very difficult for weak, average men and women to pose as angels for a protracted period. Also long repression in the ardent is not beneficial. The fish-order of human beings may wait for one another for years with impunity.

How shall a man manage the modern woman as a lover? If all modern women were alike,

this question could be answered very briefly.
But although the women of to-day sing from
a loud and dominating keynote, they possess
tones of different quality and sweetness.   When
the prevailing note of independence is sung in
a high, shrill voice, reflect calmly, O man, before
you sign away every tittle of your manhood.
There are men who like to be ruled by the
women they love; there are men who can tolerate
being dominated; and there are others who hate
the idea of being under petticoat government.

I can only tender my meagre counsel to the
third order.   The first do not need any advice.
They are quiet, tractable, somewhat feeble souls,
who are nevertheless rational and shrewd enough
to apprehend that their destiny is to be a strong
woman's husband.   They are aware of certain
limitations within themselves, which will be
counterbalanced by the virility of the woman
who condescends to honour them by asking for
their life-long attachment and contented servi-
tude.   There are a few men—perhaps not so few
as we think—who like to be bullied, oppressed,
and trodden underfoot by their lovers and wives.

Possibly Nature evolves these types for the
definite end of advancing the masculine woman;
for there is no question that a compliant spouse
is a very useful auxiliary of the Napoleonic

D

woman, born to command and conquer. The Over-Woman and the meek man are often happy together. I may say, however, that once or twice in my life I have heard the meek man swear under his breath.

The man who can tolerate a domineering lover may become reconciled to his position by the exercise of firmness and patience. He must stand up for his rights at an early stage in the courtship, or he will lose for ever his charter of freedom.

Let us suppose that his Gwendolen dislikes bull-dogs; that he wishes to keep a specimen of those unæsthetic animals; and that she has set her heart upon a cat and Pekinese terrier. Must the bull-dog be given up? I fear so, if Gwendolen makes it a point, and Horatio desires domestic concord. But Horatio must not forswear bull-dogs without protest. Let him raise an objection against cats *plus* dogs. He can endure one or the other, but not both at the same time. Let him urge that if Gwendolen cannot upon any consideration receive a bull-dog into the bosom of the family, he really cannot accept a cat as well as a Pekinese terrier.

Submit the matter to arbitration, and be firm. After all, you can make shift with a fox-terrier, if the bull-dog is not to be thought of; but do not assent to the cat as well as the Pekinese terrier. Don't be wrecked before you are out of port.

You smile at my illustration, and think it ridiculous. But I assure you that if, in the antagonism of the sexes, you cede your small privileges too easily, you will find that the Over-Woman will not leave you much to call your own in the way of liberty of action. She will treat you like a child, not unkindly; but in a maternal, fussy way that it is especially irritating to many strong-willed men. When strong women do not regard us as big children, and alternately cocker us and scold us, they look upon us as selfish brutes or contemptible fools.

The modern woman is evolving on the lines of intelligence, forcefulness, and independence, and, whether men like it or not, the absolute sway of the human male is moribund in every class except the lowest. The doll-like, insipid incarnation, still admired by some men, is hopelessly doomed to disappearance under the new conditions.

I cannot think of any phase of human evolution that is proceeding so rapidly under our eyes as the advance of woman towards sex-equality. If the modern man fails to observe this, he is lamentably deficient in observation and percep-

tion.   Men who realise and face the fact know
that they must choose a companion, and not a
plaything only.   In the long-run the good that
will accrue to men and to the race will be enor-
mous; but in the transition stage both sexes are
bound to suffer much.

We are confronted with both growth and
decay, and just as these changes are inseparable
from more or less pain in the human organism,
so are they inseparable from pain in the community.

The young generation of educated women
clamouring at the door, are no more unfeminine
or unsexed than the women of the time of Eliza-
beth, who learned Latin and talked upon intellectual subjects with men.   The same cry of
"unfeminine" was doubtless heard then.   It
has been heard in every century, and it is not
the invention of latter-day journalists, but the
age-old plaint of men, whose jealousy of
woman's progress is one of the plainest pages
of human history.

The present is the era of the man-contemning,
man-hating woman.   There is not a woman's
club in London wherein you will not hear
avowed dislike of men among a fairly large
number of the members.   What is the cause of
this seemingly unnatural attitude?   Is it a real

or a spurious contempt? In most cases it is a form of protest against life in general, with man as the scapegoat for all that is amiss in the status of woman. In some instances it is a mere fashion, a form of feminine cynicism, which means very little. Sometimes the aversion is real and deep.

Women who sincerely hate men are scarce. Those who say that they have a poor opinion of men, and a contempt for them, are somewhat numerous. The typical man-detesting woman— the true type—is not always, as depicted in fiction and the comic papers, a sort of human hybrid, with a moustache, a manly physique, and an affectation of man's clothing. She is not always an ugly woman, with an unpleasing voice, and dressed like a dowdy. On the contrary, she is sometimes beautiful and very attractive to men, though sexually abnormal.

It is singular, but true, that women of the man-despising order are often amative, and the heroines of a series of love-affairs. Frequently they have been loved devotedly; they have made easy conquests of men's hearts. We can only set it down to strange human perversity that women who are much loved, and men whom many women love, are apt to exhibit very strong sex-hostility.

Practised and hardened flirts in both sexes

usually cherish no high ideal of the opposite sex.
They have wasted the most precious thing in
life in mimic passions and spurious attachments;
they have played so long at love that love itself
has deserted them.   There is a large element of
emotional vice in flirting.   You cannot tamper
with love without suffering psychic injury.
There is, of course, harmless flirtation, and flirtation that impairs the power to love.   If you
play and trifle long with love, he will turn and
revenge himself by flying away, never to return.

The battered butterflies of women are mostly
cynical about love.   They are pests.   Having
wasted their youth in philandering, they degenerate in middle-age into stinging insects, malignant, disappointed, jealous, and delighting in
scandalous gossip.   No longer finding joy in
flitting from flower to flower, they sneer at real
passion and profess contempt for lovers.

Sometimes the man-hater is an ill-favoured
woman, a cold woman, or a shrew, who has
missed love through her own fault, or through
misfortune.   The plain woman whom men do
not desire is often a jewel that has not been
discovered by the purblind.   Often, on the other
hand, she is ill-tempered, stupid, and unattrac-
tive mentally as well as physically.

The cold woman frequently becomes a

militant man-hater, and especially so when she is beautiful. Her bosom rankles with resentment against the undiscerning fools of men who have passed her by in spite of her charms. She does not realise that exterior beauty alone is not always magnetic. If her coldness is congenital and incurable she is to be pitied, and not censured by the more fortunate.

Among the great army of the sex, the regiment of aggressively man-hating women is of full strength, and signs of the times show that it is being steadily recruited. On its banner is emblazoned, "Woe to Man"; and its call to arms is shrill and loud. These are the women who are "independent of men," a motley host, pathetic in their defiance of the first principles of Nature, but of no serious account in the biological or social sense. The women who will compose the Matriarchate of the future will not be man-haters. They will probably spoil men with yearning protective kindness, as men have tended to spoil women in the past.

A great factor in the antagonism of men towards women is the fear of the Unknown. When a savage first heard a clock strike the hour, he threw it down in a frenzy of fright, and smashed it to pieces. This dread and hatred of the mysterious and apparently inexplicable is a common human trait, not only observed among primitive folk, but prevalent in a high degree in Mayfair and Kensington, as well as in Bethnal Green.

Woman has always been associated with mystery, taboo, and sacred ritual. The holy writings of every religion, from the most primitive to the most cultured and elaborate, show very clearly how men have dreaded the influence of women in most of the affairs of life, due to the widespread attribution of beneficent magical powers to the sex.

The average modern man cannot easily rid himself of the old superstitious regard for woman. I know many men who exhibit distinct fear of women, and avoid their company as often as possible, "because they don't know how to talk to women, and don't understand them." Some of these men would be described by women as "poor dears." They are often very virile, masculine, and physically courageous men. But in the presence of woman they are tremulous, tongue-tied, and appalled.

The man who understands woman best, and fears her the least, possesses a strong trace of the feminine soul. This is not saying that he is emasculated, or feminine in an abnormal sense; he may be quite normally a man in body and mind. But he has in his brain and heart those qualities of understanding and sympathy which are more feminine than masculine. In like manner, the women who are happiest in their comprehension of men, and are described by men as good companions, either in wedlock or in friendship, have an element of masculinity in their minds and bosoms.

CHAPTER IV.

THE WAR IN WEDLOCK.

MARRYING is somewhat out of fashion nowadays, and Cassandra voices are raised against the time-honoured institution of wedlock. When we were children our parents were still young, for men and women married at an early age a few decades ago. But to-day marriage is deferred, as a shrewd man of business defers the payment of a bill upon which there is no discount. We want to secure all the enjoyment that the capital of single freedom affords, even though we regard marriage as our ultimate and almost inevitable fate.

It was not so fifty years ago. Young men and damsels married in their twenties, and often before; they were less prudent than the modern generation, more sentimental, and more hasty in this important decision. Now a man waits until he is at least thirty-five or forty, while a woman refuses to rush into the matrimonial toils at twenty. It is more difficult to get mar-

ried to-day than it was in the time of our fathers
and mothers.

The deferment of marriage is due largely to an
economic hindrance.   In the days of crinolines
the middle-class standard of living was modest,
even humble, when contrasted with the standard
of our day.   The merchant, the professional
man, and the moderately prosperous shop-keeper
often lived at the warehouse, office, or shop.
He spent very little upon ostentation.   It is one
thing to hire a gig for an occasional jaunt to
Richmond; it is another thing to keep a motor-
car and a chauffeur.

Everything in our time is more costly in the
long-run, including wives, than in the Early
Victorian period.   Cheap food and cheap clothes
do not count against the increase in rents and the
hundred-and-one expenses which are considered
essential to the keeping-up of a position of
respectability.   No one, artist, author, lawyer,
or tradesman, can afford to appear impecunious
to-day.   We are ten times more commercial
than we were sixty years ago, and the commercial spirit has invaded the sanctuary of love.
Our grandmothers recklessly married poor mer-
chants, lawyers, and doctors, and were content
to live in streets that are now considered mean
and intolerable.   To earn a living now, it is

necessary to make a continual show of monetary
success.   A man's worth is judged by his house,
his apparel, his expenditure; in fact, by everything except his higher attainments and his
virtues.

Another check upon early marriage is the
incessant attack upon that state directed by
"teachers" of all sorts, social essayists, journalists, novelists, and dramatists.   The diatribes
fired at the celibate are enough to scare them for
life from entering into unions that are described
as " slavery," " unequal," " oppressive," " para-
sitical," and " immoral."   Every publishing
season brings forth a crop of pessimistic novels,
treating the theme of unhappy wedlock in the
most sombre of hues.

Nevertheless, there are still instances of ideal
marriage.   Happy wedlock is the greatest
moralising influence in society, and the chief
felicity that life affords to men and women whose
natures are attuned to love and conjugality.
The reason why so many of us are unhappy in
marriage is because we do not regard love as
a fine art.   A capable and triumphant suitor
imagines that he can dismiss the guise of the
lover, and assume the toga of the husband after
a few months of dalliance and tenderness.   A
bride who has brought a lover to her net

imagines that he will be always reconciled to the conjugal cage, and that she has no further need for those gentle arts which she exercised during courtship.

There is more need for love-making in wedlock than in the betrothal days. God bless us all, we are children who want to be noticed, flattered, petted, and played with! As soon as a husband ceases to admire his wife for her features and her other charms, or her domestic economy, or her mental parts, or her goodness, or what not, he is losing the lover attitude and merging into a state of mere toleration. When a wife neglects those gentle offices that count for so much in daily life, and ceases to take interest in her husband's opinions and hobbies, she is forgetting that love can only be kept aglow by art and tact.

In ideal marriage there is a truce to sex-antagonism. The universal element of discord is ignored as though it had no existence. Such remarks as " How like a woman! " are not heard on the lips of the man; and his wife refrains from censures upon the opposite sex. Call it hypocrisy, if you like. Which will you choose: this state of truce with its possibilities of peace and happiness, or that strenuous life wherein sex-hostility is given full play?

Perfect conjugality depends upon adaptability, mental and physical. How seldom do a man and a woman attain the twin-joys of delight in the mind and body of one another. Is not this possible consummation within reach of more men and women?

Yes: but before ideal marriages are common men need to learn what women want, just as women need to study what men desire. How this is to be learned under the present system of social intercourse between the sexes, with its decrees against honest speech, its hundred hypocrisies, dissimulations, and lies, is more than I can answer.

The War in Wedlock is one of the fiercest conflicts waged between the sexes. It makes hells of thousands of homes; it fosters sexual vice; it paralyses the finest powers of men and women; it has a terrible effect upon the children; and it is the cause of grave mental and physical injury. Let us endeavour to understand the chief causes of warfare in the conjugal state.

A man of the ordinary stamp falls in love with a woman who consents to become his life-long partner. Both the man and the woman are often obsessed by delusions about love and marriage; they are swept along by their affections, and they think that the flood will carry them safely to a quiet haven.

What does the average man know of the soul of the woman whose head rests upon his breast and whose arms encircle him? What does he know concerning the physical nature of this human being, whose organs, functions, and desires are in so many respects widely different from his own? My answer is, "Almost nothing."

What does the woman know of the real inner life and emotions of the man to whom she has pledged herself? How much does she know of his physical life and function? My answer is again, "Almost nothing." Yet these two children of Adam have planned to live together in the closest of all human intimacies, and to bring other souls into the world!

The War in Wedlock arises most frequently from the profound ignorance of one sex concerning the other, an ignorance that is fostered by our conventions, and even commended by misguided teachers and parents. The great " one half of life," which " women should not know," is a locked volume to the maiden, who suddenly finds herself, to all intents and purposes, fettered for life to a man who can force her to his wishes, even with the use of cruelty, and still keep outside of the law of the land.

The "man of the world," the man who has "seen life," may have had a number of experiences, some beneficial and some injurious, but he has at least a certain amount of knowledge. But the knowledge that he has gained from the *demi-monde* is useless as an equipment for understanding the soul and the desires of a chaste and ignorant woman. His mind is probably pornographic; the mind of the woman is an almost white surface, with here and there a faint impression, but no more. Even if he is chaste, he is still, in the majority of cases, scarcely fit to become the sole protector of a woman's person, soul, and destiny.

To all but the most dull, unimpressionable, and imperceptive of men and women, marriage is a continual revelation. It is a revelation of oneself and of one's partner that never ceases. I know married folk whose so-called contentment is like that of two turnips growing side by side. These are not the men and women who really live. Tens of thousands of people miss life altogether. I speak now of human beings who, by heredity and habit, are forced to feel and to think. These are the mortals to whom life presents its painful problems as well as its sweetest raptures. And to them the question of how to make the best of marriage is a vital one.

Education, in its broadest sense, is one remedy for the ignorance of the sexes concerning one another; but our conception of "education" is confined to books, and has only a slight bearing upon many of the large things of life. There must be freer social intercourse between the sexes before we can diminish sex-misunderstanding and sex-antagonism. Mixed clubs of men and women are helping to break down the old fatuous barriers. Co-education in youth is another step in the right direction. Anything that hinders the segregation of the sexes tends to lessen this lack of understanding between men and women, and lends hope that the sex-union of the future will be happier than it is to-day.

We should insist that fundamental physiological facts should be taught, first lovingly in the home, and afterwards by scientific teaching in the colleges. I know that both the pornographic and the prudish persons, who swarm in every class of society, will jeer at, or veto, this proposal; and that cant in its most frantic forms must be fought before this reform is established.

All that promotes the understanding of the sexes one for the other should be encouraged in the young man and woman. Art, the drama, poetry, and fiction may be used to serve this

E

purpose. But all false art must be excluded. Biological science is of great service in revealing the mysteries of organic life, and in showing the processes of Nature in the reproduction of plants and animals. By such means we may in future time escape from the horrible welter of indecency and prudery in which we now live, and emerge as a new race of clean-minded men and women.

Marriage in the future will be more attractive to celibates than it is to-day. The contract will not be cruel in its exaction of cohabitation for persons who have ceased to love. There will be facilities for complete and honourable separation, with no hindrance to a second union, and no imputations against those who wish to sunder an insupportable rivet. When more women partially or entirely support themselves, marriage will not be so widely regarded by women as a means of subsistence. Women will marry for love; they will be in a position enabling them to marry for this natural reason, instead of for one or another of a score of reasons, such as a desire to be supported in ease and idleness, or the need of a roof, or to escape from relatives, or to avoid the reproach of old maidenhood.

There has been much discussion upon " free love" during the past thirty years. I cannot now rehearse even a small part of all that accredited writers and reformers have written and uttered on this question. Free love is for those who find any other kind of love intolerable, and I see no reason why these members of the community should be forced into the Procustean bed of indissoluble wedlock. The free union has had its trial; and we are in a better position to judge of its chances of success than even our grandfathers, when Godwin united with Mary Wollstonecraft.

Free love in communal life has not proved a victory for the advocates of the socialisation of affection. From Oneida Creek to various experiments in our country the record is invariably one of failure. On the other hand, the free unions of isolated pairs of men and women often prove happy. These are simply conjugal alliances, without religious sanction or legal registration. It is my own belief that men and women who can be happy in " free love " of this kind can also find happiness in conventional marriage. But this does not settle the question as to what shall be done for the polygamous man and the polyandous woman, who are devoid of the conjugal instinct.

Antagonism in marriage is often shown by husbands and wives who are, in their innermost hearts, attached to one another.   It is apt to be displayed, and sometimes in a violent manner, by very fervent lovers.   For a spell hate takes the place of love; the curse falls from lips that have clung in kisses, and the hand that has often soothed is raised in anger.   What a terrible transformation!   Such scenes upheave all the foundations of our fine theories, and make us pause, dismayed and shocked.

A doctor, who has had opportunities for studying human nature in various quarters of the globe, tells me that, according to his own observation, assault is quite common in married life in all classes of society.   We can scarcely dispute this statement.   Hysteria is a wide-spread disease among modern men and women, but commoner in women than in men.   The hysterical woman is often attractive, mentally and physically; she is sensitive, affectionate, impulsive, vivacious, and variable.   Most of the saints, heroines, martyrs, artists, and poetesses who have achieved great things have been more or less hysterical.   Many eminent men have also exhibited symptoms of the hysterical tendency.

Hysteria is by no means an unmitigated evil. But in certain acute manifestations it leads to "scenes" between lovers and husbands and wives, and is the cause of violent quarrels, physical violence, and even murderous assaults, especially when the man as well as the woman is affected by the loss of control over the inhibitory centres. Artistic natures are often highly hysterical, and in the unions of the artistic we have endless instances of " domestic fury." On the other hand, some of the marriages between persons of the artistic temperament have proved idylls of exalted and romantic love.

Many women—perhaps most—will tell you that the man who can, even in passion, raise his hand to a woman is an " utter brute," and that " cruelty " of this kind is unpardonable. There is no justification for such a sweeping assertion. Physical attacks upon men by women are extremely common, and every doctor who has had hospital experience will confirm this. In a large proportion of alleged cases of cruelty on the part of a husband, the wife is the aggressor. I know a man in a good position in society who relates that he has been bitten, scratched, struck in the face, and kicked by the women he has loved. Thousands of men could tell the same tale. Among the working class men are often taken to the infirmaries suffering from wounds inflicted by their wives in fits of temper. We do not hear of these cases, because if a man were to charge a woman with assault, his evidence would be received with jeers, and it is probable that a facetious magistrate would advise him to go home, and not to be a fool, etc.

An irritable, excitable, strong-willed woman will often incite a man to "assault" her. A dispute arises, and she flies into a passion, upbraids, cries, and denounces her husband in stinging terms. If he goes from the room, she follows him, railing still louder, and annoying him to the point of madness. Unless the man has colossal power of control, his nervous irritability breaks loose, and he slaps the woman or holds her wrists, and tells her not to behave like a child. The woman then shrieks that the man is a hooligan and a brute, and that she does not care if all the neighbours know it. Very often the woman is the first to strike; and it is absurd to pretend that a robust woman, under the influence of anger, cannot hurt or injure a man.

I shall not be in the least surprised if, after reading this, many of my critics accuse me of deliberately defending or advocating wife-beating. But I do not intend to refrain from plain-speaking under fear of misconception. The facts are lamentable, but they are facts to be set down "without prejudice." We hear terrible accusations of brutality and cruelty against men.

We hear very little of the frightful provocation that men receive from women before they lose control. In justice one must admit that a nerve-tired, much-tried woman, continually worried by physical ailments, a large family, and a difficult husband should have due allowance made for her explosions of wrath. But what of the pampered, wealthy, spoiled women, whose irritability arises from nervous breakdown occasioned by luxury and *ennui*? These are to be pitied, but not excused.

In the War in Wedlock many women act with deliberate cruelty, and display the same "brutal" impulses as men. "Hard words break no bones," it is true; but biting tongues stab the heart, and the effect of their stabs is more lasting and painful than blows. Some women indulge periodically in "rows" and "scenes." The outbursts are sudden and violent, like an August thunderstorm, and the cause is often difficult to trace. After the tempest the woman is often penitent and loving. At heart she is a good woman; and the man who has been abused or beaten should take her in his arms, and confess that he ought to have been more patient and tactful.

It is a Herculean labour of patience to manage a dominating, contentious, and obstinate woman.

Most men do not attempt the task. A phleg-
matic husband has neither the inclination nor the
energy for such a stupendous business. His
ideal is peace at any price, and when his wife
fumes, he folds his arms and listens in silence.
He will yield almost any point in order to secure
peace. A choleric man, with a masterful disposition, essays to manage such a woman, and
occasionally succeeds. Most often he fails, and
" scenes " arise with a sort of rhythmical recur-
rence, and continue until death or a mutual
separation severs the torturing link.

A modern woman of the contentious type is
often amenable to reason and love. If she will
only listen quietly—a process that is painful to
her—you may firmly, rationally, and kindly con-
vince her that she is not always in the right; that
you have no desire to play the bully, nor any
intention of allowing her to bully you; that you
will compromise on certain points, but not on
others; and that you respect her, and gave the
fullest pledge of that respect when you chose
her from among all the women known to you
as the mate after your own heart. A woman
who will not listen to such a manifesto must be
endured, or dismissed from your life. Probably
you will be unable to cut the knot, for even the
most contentious, fractious, and intractable of

women possess subtle and talismanic attractions
for certain men.   Nothing is left then but to
suffer and be strong.

We are often told that there should be no question of " management " in marriage.   No doubt
there are instances of husbands and wives whose
managing of one another is so slight, or so
extremely tactful, that the process is not apparent.
But of the mass of human beings in wedlock this
is not so.   There is usually a predominant
partner.   No man should feel ashamed of being
directed in most of his affairs by a wise, loving,
and faithful wife.   But few men can live hap-
pily with a female drill-sergeant.

To say that there is no managing in marriage
is to deny one of the plainest facts of life.   Most
women are born managers of men.   And if men
want to retain any of that freedom, which is at
present their alleged exclusive privilege, they
must learn how to manage women.

Let me take horse-breaking as an illustration,
an art in which I have gained some experience.
A good trainer of young horses should never
blunder in his psychology.   He must study his
colt as one studies the idiosyncrasy of a child.
Some horses are prone to sulk; some are given to
kicking; some are gentle, but obstinate, some
are hot-tempered, and so on.   One fractious

horse can be cured by judicious severity; another will be ruined by the whip. Broadly speaking, in the management of men, women, children, servants and animals, the whip should be a symbol rather than an instrument. The whole art of control is in psychological observation and tact. Brute force is usually, perhaps always, the clumsiest and least effective method. I know that force is very English; but it is not argument and it is seldom reasonable.

I have said that women are born-managers of men. Naturally, the maternal duties make them directors and disciplinarians. But they are mostly rule-of-thumb managers, and not thoughtful students of human nature, with a scientific method. They rely on force, just as most men rely on force; but a woman's exercise of force differs from a man's exercise of force. A woman uses her force largely through an appeal to the best that is in man, and she has learned how to employ this force with tyrannous effect. When a woman has done wrong, she wins back her ascendancy over the outraged and injured husband by appealing to his protective instincts. She weeps; she uses rare art in exciting pity, and only the callous can resist her. You cannot trample on that clinging, trembling, sobbing creature, whose tears wet your neck, and whose little heart throbs against your bosom. You give in. Ignominiously? Yes, sometimes, because she is often entirely in the wrong, and is just an artful, naughty, spoilt child, who is determined that she will win you over.

Even strong-minded women who indignantly repudiate a suggestion of " wheedling," know quite well in their heart of hearts that their final appeal to the protective, cherishing instinct of a man is a form of wheedling, an exercise of force. Woman's last attack is always on this highly vulnerable part of a man's emotional being. There are occasions when a man must preserve a front of steel to these attacks. To yield, when instinct and conviction urge stern refusal, is to commit an error that may darken the whole of life for the man as well as the woman.

It is always well for a man to remember of what plastic stuff he is made. The fine delicate fingers of the woman for whom he possesses an infatuation can mould him into a shape that he may not be able to recognise as his own image. This is why many great men, with high ambitions and ideals, philosophers, reformers, artists, statesmen, and soldiers have remained single, and avoided the risk of this moulding at the hands of women. Have not all the great religious teachers recognised that the married man's chief desire is how he shall please his wife?

"Woman is essentially implacable, like the cat," writes Nietzsche, "however well she may have assumed the peaceable demeanour." Irascibility, "touchiness," and an apparent liking for wordy combat are very common womanly failings. The cause is often physical, and connected with the very complex sexual life of woman. Men should be patient with women, for women suffer in bearing the race from girlhood to advanced middle-age.

On the other hand, a show of force, even a touch of cruelty, is necessary in the management of certain hysterical women. It is often insincerity that causes women to accuse men of roughness. A reasonable amount of harshness frequently appeals to a refractory woman more than gentle suasion. The men most loved by women are not often the gentlest of men. The female expects a measure of roughness in the male. But the man who can be rough must also be kind at heart. "The stroke of death is as a lover's pinch, which hurts and is desired," says Shakespeare's Cleopatra.

There is plenty of evidence to prove that women do not, as a whole sex, resent judicious harshness in a lover. They know well themselves how to inflict mental pain upon men, and do not shrink from doing so. When men reverse the process a sensible woman is not surprised. She may even be highly gratified. There is a Russian proverb, "A dear one's blows hurt not long." In parts of Hungary peasant women do not believe that they are loved until their husbands give them the first box on the ear. Most women, if they are honest, will admit that they like to be subjugated now and then by a strong man. The breaking down of a woman's natural instinct of resistance by a vehement lover is a process that few women resist for long, or afterwards resent. Every romantic girl dreams of being abducted by a powerful man, who sternly commands, but, at the same time, is ready to risk danger and pain in her protection. The universal rôle of women in courtship is that of the pursued, even when pursuit is a tame rehearsal of actual marriage by force and capture.

No man can hope for success in love or happiness in wedlock if he makes light of the fundamental needs of women, and fails to study them closely. W. S. Gilbert is quite right:

Every Jack must study the knack
If he wants to make sure of his Jill.

Be warned, however, that what will please the masculine type of woman will probably affront the tender, feminine type. There is a good deal of luck in love; but there is also much need for science. Love, like fly-fishing, looks easy enough. You try it, and find out your mistake.

Most women are pleased and flattered by the deference of their husbands, but some women much prefer a man with robust asperity. If you cannot discover which attitude appeals to the woman of your choice, you are wanting in discernment. But, then, woman, with her tendency to variability, often changes from day to day, and what pleases her in the morning may offend her at night. Women certainly keep us very busy studying to delight them, and sometimes all our efforts are in vain.

A little coldness, a little neglect, or an excitation of the instinct of jealousy are often beneficial when a woman is petulant, fractious, and much concerned with the fact that she is a woman. She will not hesitate to discipline you by such methods, if you fail in pleasing her. Therefore, apply her own tactic. If she still cares for you, she will change her mood and come to her senses, although she may at first make a display of sheer indifference.

Be not over-kind when a young wife sulks and puts you into Coventry. Let her alone for a while. Don't go up to her in a supplicating attitude, unless you want a stinging snub. Go to your club, or take a woman friend to the theatre.

It all sounds beautifully simple!

CHAPTER V.

THE FEUD IN THE FAMILY.

MANY dissensions arise in family life between the parents concerning the upbringing of children. These disagreements are likely to increase under the new conditions, because the daughter in revolt is a very wilful and resolute young person. She is apt to set both parents at defiance, and to cause discord between them. Under the moribund family order the daughter is, to a large extent, sacrificed for the advancement of the son and for the comfort of the father and mother. A girl's vocation is marriage, and one need not be educated and highly trained for domestic life. That has been the basis of parental control of daughters.

But the modern young woman is changing all that. She talks of a life of independence; she often wishes to escape from the home, and to earn a living for herself; and she scouts the idea that marriage is the sole end and aim of a woman's life.

Among the prosperous middle-class at least twice as much is spent upon the education of sons as upon that of daughters. Among the lower middle-class there is not much to expend upon the education of either boys or girls, but even in this status the boys as a rule have a better schooling than the girls. Daughters are rebelling against this inequality. They demand the same chances in life as their brothers, and if these chances are denied them, they are not unnaturally discontented.

When men talk of the intellectual incapacity of women, they usually lose sight of the fact that women have been debarred from the exercise of their capacity. For a long time to come women will have to fight against the prejudice of men in this respect; and the war will be waged bitterly in the family circle. Even Nietzsche, the hero of a school of young "Intellectuals" of both sexes, has written monstrous nonsense upon clever women and woman's aptitude for learning. This demi-god of the intensely-diverting admirers of the doctrines of *Beyond Good and Evil*, is unstinting in his sneers at the woman with brains. "When a woman has scholarly inclinations there is generally something wrong with her sexual nature." Women are to be treated in "Oriental style"; and the

F

men who approve of sex-equality are described by Nietzsche as " masculine shallowpates."

Men have said in all ages: "Woman is stupid; therefore do not waste time in educating her." And women, accepting the opinions of men as the line of least resistance, have actually played the part of being stupid in order to please their fathers, brothers, and husbands. Nowadays women are up in arms against this system. It is high time for rebellion. But this revolt does not conduce to the peace of the home. I can point to a score of families wherein this feud is raging at the present time. *Ann Veronica*, by H. G. Wells, is a true picture of the struggle that women are making against the absolutism of the parent.

The British Papa is one of the causes of this warfare. He is paying for the sins of his sex and his ancestors, and one cannot help feeling a little sorry for him. Worthy soul, his breast is in a fearful flutter! Maud has joined the Suffragettes; Grace has left home, and insists upon earning a living as typist; Agnes is intellectual and "advanced"; she is a Fabian, and talks terrible social heresies. Poor papa feels the solid foundation of his villa at Balham heaving beneath him, and sees all his preconceptions of the proper sphere of woman toppling about

his bald crown.   Truly, this is a situation full
of pathos.   It is so old, so very common; and
yet the papas of each succeeding generation
never grow used to it.

My dear British Papa, though one-half of my
brain recognises the sadness of your position,
the other half bids me rejoice that you are being
set at defiance.   You have had a long, long
reign as domestic pacha, and in your crass unin-
telligence you have committed great wrong.
You have kept your womenfolk under lock
and key; you have discouraged your daughters
from all forms of self-expression except the
maternal, and hindered the development of
women in a hundred ways.

In this matter the British Papa has been
assisted by his more or less docile ally, the British
Mamma.   Woman has always aided and abetted
man in the suppression of Woman.   A woman
here and there has tried to assert her rights in
the face of both masculine and feminine inhibitions; but the bulk of women, living dependently
upon men for a means of subsistence, have been
forced to obey the leadership of man.   The
process has given rise to antipathy between the
sexes, both overt and covert.

Parents are conspirators against their daughters' freedom.   They may be unconscious of

the conspiracy, and their aim may be the safe-
guarding of the brood. Nevertheless, the
object is to set daughters aside as beings entirely
different from sons, and to rear them in a system
of harem-like seclusion. The knowledge which
is purposely withheld from daughters is precisely
that knowledge of which they, as potential
mothers of the race, stand most in need. The
tragedies that arise from the ignorance of women
are so common that a dispassionate onlooker is
moved to wonder whether the conventional upbringing of the sex is a fantasy born in the brains
of lunatics. I rarely converse on serious subjects with women without hearing a history of
suffering and error directly traceable to the way
in which they were educated in the home and
the school.

The Advanced Daughter, with all her faults
of priggishness and a lack of consideration for
the prejudices of old-fashioned parents and relatives, is a more promising and altogether finer
type than the bread-and-butter misses of the last
generation. She is better fitted as the companion of intelligent men; she is likely to bear
healthier children, and to train them rationally,
and she is of greater service as a citizen. Her
rampant attitude is somewhat repellent, but this
is inevitable. She is out on strike; her mood

is defiant, pugnacious, assertive. She belongs
to the next age, and she is a fanatical pioneer.

The Advanced Daughter insists upon her
right to a sound education. She refuses to
spend her time in dressing and practising arts
for the captivation of men. As soon as possible
she escapes from the home environment, goes
into the world, lives in her own flat or apart-
ments, earns her living, seeks the company of
intellectual and serious men and women, and
erects the standard of Liberty. Her manner
with men is apt to be patronising, and she is
anxious to make men apprehend that she can do
without them. She is, however, susceptible to
love, and when she falls in love, she is not half-
hearted, but frank in her attachment.

A young woman who resolves to live her own
life has to pay the penalty of revolt. She will
suffer in breaking away from home-ties and
influences, especially if she is attached to her
parents. Her father counsels, commands, and
threatens; her mother weeps upon her neck.
The Advanced Daughter is deeply moved; but
she is resolved, and she goes her own way. A
vast undiscovered country is before her; she is
led on by a fascination partly made up of fear
and partly of curiosity.

When I see these earnest maidens setting forth

from Tooting, with the light of wonder in their eyes and their lips firm-set, I am reminded of Santa Teresa wandering out of Avila to seek persecution in the country of the Moors. Voices from the wilderness lure them; great vistas open before their gaze; and they go out to face life's brunts and to taste its joys.

The Advanced Daughter is nurtured upon Ibsen, Bernard Shaw, Nietzsche, Graham Wallas, and Fabian tracts. Ideas are seething in her busy little brain. She is desperately intellectual. One day she tells you that she is prepared to die for the cause of Women's Suffrage. Next week she will be immersed in economics, or vegetarianism, or free love. She theorises in season and out, and sees the world as a vast theatre for her social reforms. Her untiring energy impels her to meetings, debates, lectures, classes, and gatherings of youthful and very cocksure " Intellectuals." She absorbs " views " as a sponge absorbs water. Her tongue is glib and faster than her thoughts, which are often inchoate. She will solve you half, at least, of the riddles of the universe.

" I don't mean to marry," she says, with a ring of disdain. " I want to live my own life." She regards wives as " chattels " or " squaws." She only admires man " on the intellectual side,"

and she tries to disguise her sex-attractions by
dressing dowdily, neglecting her hair, wearing
square-toed boots, and assuming inelegant poses.
But she contrives, nevertheless, to attract men
of a certain type.   Her admirers are something
like herself, and that is why they understand
her and know her blind side.   They are not like
the clumsy Philistines who treat her deferen-
tially because of her sex.

The Advanced Daughter's chosen men-com-
panions are the adroitest flatterers in the world.
They lead up to intimate topics by highly
intellectual discussions upon Bernard Shaw, the
Court Theatre, the Budget, and the compulsory
cultivation of waste lands, in which they permit
the Advanced Daughter to roundly contradict,
correct, and instruct them.   They sit at the feet
of their monitress in respectful attention, and
artfully wedge in compliments upon her vast
superiority to the average woman, her intellectual courage, her example to the frivolous of her
sex, and her splendid unconventional morality.

It is an interesting spectacle, this philandering
of the young "Intellectuals." They would deny
that they are making love; but the whole ruse
is transparent.   The Advanced Daughter pre-
tends that she hates to be admired for her eyes
or her hair; the Advanced Son knows, however,

that sooner or later she will resent this indifference to her physical charms, and he studies how
to praise her person by the intellectual method.
Sometimes a strong, healthy rascal of a wooer
comes along, grips the Advanced Daughter's
waist, carries her off, and utterly subdues her
by his animal force and physical attractions.
For, after all, the Advanced Daughter is a
descendant of Eve.   And as Kipling says, "The
colonel's lady and Judy O'Grady are sisters
under their skin."

The escape from home life and its trammels
has been made easier in many large towns by
the establishment of clubs for women, and clubs
admitting both men and women.   These institutions were unknown about thirty years ago,
but they are now common in London.   Their
influence, on the whole, has been for good.
Mixed clubs improve the manners of men, and
teach them more about women; while they tend
to dispel some of the silliness of women, and
to break down the sex-barrier.   Scandals arise
occasionally, but scandals also arise in nunneries
and chapel congregations.

Women now use their clubs as men use them.
They have their smoking-rooms; they drink
wine, and sometimes whisky-and-soda.   The
Advanced Daughter is almost always a club-

woman, and some women spend hours of every
day in their clubs.   I have not heard that husbands and babies are neglected as a consequence,
though such instances may have arisen.   At any
rate, mixed clubs have brought men and women
together on an equal footing, and tended to
lessen the conventional segregation of the sexes.

An Advanced Daughter says: "Come to my
club."   You obey, and you are entertained at
tea in the smoking-room, and sometimes
allowed to smoke a pipe.   Your hostess talks
cleverly, if not profoundly; you feel at home—
far more at home than in a drawing-room—and
the time passes pleasantly and profitably.   The
more of these clubs the better for men and
women.   They will aid in lessening sex antagonism.

The clubs for women only are not so wholesome as the mixed clubs.   Whenever those of
the same sex get together, some of their less
pleasing qualities manifest themselves.   Men
tend to a freedom and a frankness, which would
be salutary where they decent and serious, while
women assembled together talk hypocritically
and infect one another with feminine morbidities.

As part of the management of the Modern
Woman, I advise fathers and husbands to encourage their womenfolk to join a mixed club.

A woman constantly mewed up in the home becomes narrow in her outlook, irritable, and subject to discontent and depression. The mass of women living in the suburbs and in country towns suffer from a want of social intercourse.

CHAPTER VI.

THE STRIFE IN BREADWINNING.

THE battle of the sexes, in obtaining the means of subsistence, has assumed a menacing aspect. Men complain that they are being ousted from professions and trades by women, and that women's labour is lowering the standard of wages. "In a short time," they say, " there will be no occupations left for men except the hardest and roughest kinds of toil." For a long period men jealously guarded against this encroach of women into fields of industry, but women entered the fields one by one, and now they are rushing in everywhere.

This change is very significant. It demonstrates the widespread desire of women to become economically independent of men; and it denotes that the modern woman is by no means a degenerate creature, but one possessed of a high degree of energy and a great capacity for work. Some of us will remember the days when a hundred forms of employment were barred to women. We can recall the bitter, even brutal, opposition offered by men to the admission of women to the medical profession. The behaviour of men at this time was stupid and cowardly. We shall probably witness a repetition of this conduct when women demand to practise law.

Why should not women be solicitors and barristers? Miss Christabel Pankhurst, a woman of great intellectual ability and of fine character, is fully capable of holding her own with any of our counsels. The time is coming when women will sit with men on the judicial bench. And one day our grandchildren will see a woman as Premier.

Women are now employed in all kinds of occupations that were once closed to them. Those who have benefited most by the innovation are the large employers of labour, who offer wages to women which men would spurn. Women are frightfully sweated in almost every profession and trade, and they are only beginning to realise that they must combine for the protection of their interests.

I am entirely opposed to the view of Bebel and his school that woman should be practically absolved from labour. Half of women's troubles are due to an insufficient employment of their brains and hands. If more women worked, many of the problems of society would be solved, and women would be healthier and

happier.   The upper and the rich middle-class
women are usually parasites of man.   Their one
trade is to please men—a very proper and Oriental occupation, according to Nietzsche.   Women
who have other objects in life besides " adorning
the home," and increasing the population, rebel
against this view.   Child-bearing and rearing do
not absorb the whole of a woman's energies.
Besides, many women are unmarried, and have
not enough domestic duties to fill their lives.

Many women are quite capable of physical
toil, and they are better in body and mind when
using their muscles han when living in idleness.
The most beautiful women and the most robust
I ever saw are the field-labourers of Northern
Portugal.   One cannot travel in that district
without gaining conviction that these women are
gayer in spirit, more healthy and well-developed,
and more æsthetic than the fine ladies of Oporto
and Lisbon.   I am not defending the ill-
remunerated labour of our chain-and-nail makers
in merry England, but I challenge the view that
woman is naturally unfit for muscular exertion.

Sex-rivalry in breadwinning must be studied
as a phase of sex-antagonism.   So long as men
were the sole breadwinners, they owned the
sovereign position in the home.   A wife who is
wholly dependent for food, shelter, and clothing

upon the earnings of a husband is a species of pauper. Her sole asset is her power of attracting and holding the man who provides for her and the children. Naturally, the Nietzschean philosophers would keep her in this more or less splendid bondage.

Does it not strike the male opponents of the employment of women in business that, in spite of the seeming rivalry, men are, in the long run, but little injured by the competition? Most men desire wives, and more men would marry early in life had they the means of supporting a family. If women workers threaten to lessen the number of industrial openings for men, they also bring grist to the domestic mill, and thus the competition is freed from one of its chief menaces. Obviously, a wife with a trade costs less to keep than one who contributes nothing towards the household expenses.

The stage is a profession that affords an illustration of the economic equality of men and women. Actors are often married to actresses, and both the husband and the wife support themselves. The system works well enough not only in this profession, but in many others.

Men and women who work side by side tend to lose a part of their natural antagonism. It is most important that women should be occupied;

otherwise they grow fretful, depressed, and morbid. Give your wife plenty of work to do, and let this be a rule in your policy of management. Not long ago an elderly husband remarked to me, " While my wife was having babies she was quite contented and happy, and found full employment. Now that the children have grown up, she is capricious, dissatisfied with life, and full of worries."

Women should work hard, but care should be taken that they do not overtax their strength. Men can amuse themselves with hobbies and games, as I have said before; but women are singularly unresourceful in this matter. They have only needlework to fall back upon as an occupation for long hours of leisure, and needlework is not a wholesome employment. A woman who knits or crochets cannot escape from herself, as a man does when he plays at golf or goes fly-fishing. She thinks too much about her " soul," her trials, her fading beauty, the defects of her husband, and a host of matters. Needlework is provocative of " nerves." This employment is compatible with deep, serious introspection, and most women are far too introspective by nature.

Encourage your wife to work in a garden. Let her dig, and hoe, and use a lawn-mower.

Housework is very good for women. I know ladies who have found themselves in much better health after dismissing one or all of their servants, and undertaking the work of the home. The middle-class woman is apt to love idleness. As a result she grows bored, ill-tempered, and hard to live with. When a woman has nothing to employ her mind, she becomes vividly conscious of the awful fact that she is a woman.

If a woman will not work, you should encourage her to play. Let her join hockey and tennis clubs; teach her to scull, fence, box—anything that will develop her physical strength and tone up her nervous system. A want of exercise is the bane of many women, especially in town life. I never go into the company of the average overfed, dyspeptic, neurasthenic middle-class women without longing to set them to do three hours' turnip-hoeing every day. It is necessary to emphasise woman's need to work and to play. An idle wife is an unhealthy wife, and an ailing woman is often very bad company. The bicycle has proved a great boon to women. By all means persuade your wife to cycle with you as often as possible. Keep her away from "fancy needlework" by all the means in your power. Insist firmly upon the cold or tepid bath daily, and see that she takes brisk exercise out of doors in all weathers. Many women are like pampered cats, they love to lie overwarm, and they are fastidious in their diet. If you take such a creature into your home, you will have an ill time with " nerves," hysteria, mental depression, headaches, various forms of malaise, nagging, and doctors' bills.

In all " civilised " countries, the struggle in breadwinning drives a large number of women into that very ancient profession which we scarcely care to name. The " social evil " is a flagrant example of the conflict of the sexes. Its chief cause, on the authority of eminent European investigators, is the dependent position of woman. There is undoubtedly " the courtesan type "; but I think that Lombroso and other writers have over-stated the widespread tendency of women to adopt this profession naturally. The source is principally economic. My personal inquiry has been fairly wide, and my conviction is that poverty is most often the dire incentive.

No very wide distinction can be drawn between the dependent woman who, without real affection, solves the problem of her poverty by marriage, and the woman who enters the profession of mercenary polyandry. Both are victims; both are impelled by the same basic

G

economic need.   Loveless wedlock for subsistence is the fate of tens of thousands of women. It is a fate that will not be endured for ever. The Woman Movement is principally a battle for the economic equality of men and women, and when women are economically free, only the congenital, courtesan types, and the idle degenerates will sell themselves to men.

The women who resort to this traffic may be taken as symbols of sex-antagonism.   They are outlaws at war with men, upon whom they prey.   Men say that they are "a necessity"; but men take the utmost care that these necessary ministers to their desires shall receive no social recognition for their services.   On the contrary, the courtesan is doomed to live in a state of helotry.   She is treated with ignominy, even cruelty; she is the loneliest woman in the community.   Women avoid her as a pest, and men are rarely her friends on an equal basis.   It was different in ancient Greece.

This great, neglected question, so little understood by the sociologist, so scrupulously avoided by the average man and woman, will engage the most capable minds in the society of the future. It is a question of the deepest importance. That is why we shirk or obfuscate it.   The evil will probably live, in one form or another, to the end of time; but it will be greatly lessened when the monetary dependence of women is removed.   I assure women that one of the soundest methods of establishing greater sexual purity is not preaching chastity, nor suppression, nor police intervention, nor rescue work, but the insistence upon opening out employment for women at wages that will lift them above want.

CHAPTER VII.

THE BATTLE IN POLITICS.

THE Christian English gentleman, reared in the doctrine of St. Paul concerning the subjection of women, can scarcely imagine a state in which women are the directors of legislation, the heads of families, the dominant sex. He tells you that such a condition is unthinkable; it never has been, and never will be. The average Christian English gentleman is, however, not addicted to deep reflection upon social problems, and in nine cases out of ten, he knows next to nothing of the moral codes, manners, and marriage customs of other nations. His eye is fixed upon England, and usually upon one little corner of it. He talks about "thinking Imperially." He is anything but cosmopolitan in his outlook on human life.

Men of this parochial bias vehemently oppose the elevation of women, and fear the rule of woman as a final social catastrophe. They are ignorant of the fact that, among many of the most civilised of ancient races, the Matriarchate was the custom of the country for hundreds of year; and that the headship of woman is in existence to-day among many peoples of the earth. Among the Etruscans, Athenians, Campanians, Arcadians, Lycians, and other communities the women were the directors. Men assumed the names of heir wives upon marriage; they yielded all their possessions to the woman, asking only for simple maintenance, and a decent burial at the end of their lives. The primitive Teutons adopted the matriarchal system. To-day the custom survives in Malabar; among the Khassias, the Pani Kotches, and certain tribes of British India. My good Christian English gentleman, *do* try to think Imperially! These things are done under the British flag.

For long ages paternity was regarded as of small account. Physiologically, it is of quite secondary importance. Race and family sprang from the mother, not the father. The highly intelligent Nairs of Malabar afford to-day an example of the modern Matriarchate. "No people have more fully appreciated the maternal family nor developed it more logically than the Nairs," writes Élie Reclus, in *Primitive Folk*.

It is curious to note that, under the

matriarchal system, men complained, as women complain to-day, of the subordinate position they occupied. We find also that men spoke with formal deference to women, adopting the kind of courtesy which survives among men to-day towards women, but from a different motive, for it was the deference of the owned towards the owner. In Mexico we read of a father who could not sell any produce, such as corn, without the consent of his daughter, who kept house for him. To-day in France, where the mother has far more authority than in England, we find traces of the matriarchal rule.

Under the patriarchal system, woman lost her superior position, and suffered also physically. No longer expected to labour side by side with men, she became less robust. Her worst state of physical deterioration is seen in the higher middle class of Europe to-day among the corset-wearing, nervous, dyspeptic types that abound in all large cities. Christianity is partly responsible for the institution of the modern patriarchal system, and under the rule of men, the position of women became subordinate, and wholly dependent. Both systems have their evils; but one or the other is inevitable, in spite of all our dreams of true equality of the sexes. The ascendancy of woman may be the new state into which we are passing. A revived Matriarchate has terrors for some men, probably for the vast majority. But I know many thoughtful men who anticipate the change and experience no fear.

Man's jealousy of woman has been fought and overcome in many relations. Is it not quite possible that men in the future will gladly relinquish all the cares of office and the control of family affairs to their women-folk? It is certainly not an unthinkable condition. Women are battling in the present time with a zeal and indomitable energy which must make the judicious reflect. The Feminist Movement is not local and sporadic; it is permeating the Western Continents, and has reached the countries of Islam. According to Pierre Loti, it has penetrated the Turkish harems; and a gentleman who has travelled much in Turkey tells me that the women of the country are in sympathy with the ideals of advanced English women. Even in Spain, where Moorish traditions survive, women are awakening; and the Spanish woman once aroused is the incarnation of revolt. At a great industrial struggle in Barcelona, a few years ago, the strikers were led by a girl of eighteen, who showed remarkable powers of organisation and leadership.

It may be urged that many great thinkers have been anti-feminist. Many great minds believed in astrology, witchcraft, magic, and other exploded superstitions and myths. On the other hand, there is a long list of men of eminent culture, from Plato and Tacitus to John Stuart Mill, who have pleaded for the recognition of woman's fitness for other duties besides child-bearing and the management of the house. "This sex, which we keep in obscurity and domestic work," writes Plato, in his *Republic*, "is it not fitted for nobler and more elevated functions? Are there no instances of courage, wisdom, advance in all the arts?" Plutarch counselled that women should be educated equally with men, and claimed intellectual and moral equality. Seneca was also a feminist.

And yet the average man in England is aghast at the prospect of giving women a Parliamentary vote, while the idea of extending legislative office to women arouses his derision or anger. Unfortunately, the average Englishman is as much astray in his appraisement of the potentialities of women as the two arch-Philistine apostles of misogyny, Schopenhauer and Nietzsche. The influence of these two thinkers has had baneful effect upon the judgment of certain of the young Intellectuals of to-day.

Schopenhauer's famous essay on *Woman* is the outpouring of a pessimistic sensualist who had missed love. The mother of the philosopher married without affection; she was described as "without heart and soul." Schopenhauer was never in love. His amours were those of a specialist in sensuality, and he left an account of his erotic adventures, which were not intended for publication. I yield to none in admiration for this genius, whose literary style alone is a continual joy, and whose theories are of the deepest interest. But Schopenhauer was a sheer Philistine in his attitude towards women.

Friedrich Nietzsche, a savage anti-feminist, was temperamentally akin to Schopenhauer. He knew but little of women and less of love. Many of his moral opinions and metaphysical meanderings are very instructive and entertaining. He is not a transcendent thinker, still less a god of intellect. Nietzsche quite failed to perceive the present evolution of women. His views were Oriental and sensual, and concerning women he expressed himself with brutal ignorance. He takes George Sand and Madame de Staël as the ideal emancipated women, set up as models by women, and knocks them down as "counter arguments against feminine emancipation and autonomy." These illustrious women were highly erratic geniuses, with all the imperfections and morbidities of the male genius. They are rarely cited by women as ideal types of womanhood.

"There is stupidity in this movement" (the freeing of women) writes Nietzsche; " an almost masculine stupidity, of which a well-reared woman—who is always a sensible woman—might be heartily ashamed. . . . Woman must be preserved, cared for, protected, and indulged, like some delicate, strangely wild, and often pleasant domestic animal." Men who think that woman is something more than a "dangerous cat," and "a pleasant domestic animal," are described by the courteous metaphysician as the "idiotic friends and corrupters of woman amongst the learned asses of the masculine sex."

When I want to laugh, I read Nietzsche's ravings about women in *Beyond Good and Evil*. His diatribes are as entertaining as the utterances of certain Advanced Daughters, who speak of man as "the enemy," and lay about them with a flail immediately "man" appears upon the stage.

Balzac, one of the profoundest students of the human heart, said: "A woman that has received a masculine education possesses the most brilliant and fertile qualities with which to secure the happiness of her husband and herself." But even Balzac was infected with the Oriental feeling towards women. He forbade his own nieces from reading his novels, with the exception of *Ursule Mirouët*, which he wrote expressly for them—fearing to enlighten them upon life because they were women. Balzac does not lie, as do nine out of ten novelists, about women's passions, and therein he is illuminating; but he appears to have guarded against a broadening " masculine education " for the women of his own kin.

Woman has been deified as the Mother of God, worshipped as queen, revered as priestess, honoured as teacher, respected and protected for her maternal function. Why should she be debarred from serving the State as a maker of laws? There is no logical answer to this question. The reply of sex-antagonism is: " She would become unsexed." No man considers himself unsexed by following the occupation of a draper, a cook, a nurse, a tailor, or a confectioner, employments which could be well undertaken by women. But every silly clown of a fellow begins to cackle when a cultured and capable woman claims the right to take part in the control of a municipality or a state.

In the battle for moral, intellectual, and political freedom excesses have always been committed. Emancipation is not won by platitudes, but by vehement measures, and often by violent revolt. Women, smarting under a sense of injustice, often exhibit sex-hostility in an extreme form. The shallow onlooker of the male sex declares that the irate women on the platform, and the women who resort to physical force, are to be judged as unfit for a share in the framing of the laws of their country. The modern woman, with a passionate political bias, and the conviction that she is defrauded of a common human right, is no more ridiculous in her manifestations of dissatisfaction than men under similar outbreaks. The most ridiculous figure in the present war of women for the Suffrage is the grotesquely implacable Mr. Asquith, whose rampant sex-antagonism blinds him to a score of fatal issues that will arise through his false show of firmness. A tactful politician would have received not one, but half a dozen deputations of Suffragist women, on the simple ground of expediency. Mr. Asquith, posing as the Strong Man, is a spectacle to arouse Titanic laughter. He has done more to injure the Liberal cause than any politician of modern times.

I am no advocate of rioting and disorder. But, in the name of common fairness, how can we blame women for resorting to the time-honoured custom of warfare when other measures fail?

We pride ourselves on being a martial race, and our jingoes insist that the militarist spirit should be fostered. And, in a hundred instances, Englishmen have gained their ends and brought governments to their knees by the method of mob-compulsion. A notable example is the Gin Riots of 1736, when loyal Britons shouted "No gin, no king!" This noble cause was fought because the excise duty on the national nectar had been raised to twenty shillings per gallon. For two years the outraged populace rioted, and the Guards were called out to quell the mobs. Sir Joseph Jekyll, the framer of the Bill, was threatened with his life, and sixty soldiers protected his house from the incensed people. These demonstrations and riotings were successful; the Gin Act was repealed, and the public won by means of violent agitation. Would the gin-drinkers have gained the day if they had relied upon pacific and "constitutional" methods? I believe not.

The Women's Suffrage campaign is, after all,

of quite as great importance as cheap gin agita-
tions. For fifty years constitutional means have
been employed by women, and for fifty years
men have flouted the petitioners, and deluded
them with specious promises. In the hour of
exasperation, after extreme provocation, women
are using force. It would be more than can
be expected of human nature if they acted
otherwise. Has not Mr. Balfour declared that
there is a limit to the patience of an outraged
public? In this encounter women have shown
less antagonism than men. For half a century
they have waited patiently for the right to vote.

The lesson of the Suffrage war is that women
possess a very remarkable power of organisation, an ingenuity in tactic, a supreme zeal, and
a high degree of courage. Delicately-born,
refined, and cultured women have suffered gibes,
insults, and imprisonment, and even assault,
while men have looked on complacently, and
muttered the old cant about " unsexed women."
As well endeavour to stem the tide of an ocean
as to thwart the irresistible workings of human
evolution. The times portend a widespread
uplifting of the status of woman. There are
palpable signs that human evolution in the
Western nations is proceeding more rapidly
among the females than the males. Physically,

the women are becoming stronger and taller. Intellectually, they are progressing with wonderful speed.

The fear of petticoat rule and the intellectual superiority of women is deep-rooted in the breast of man. But the roots are slackening their hold. Men are learning that a beautiful body is no compensation for a childish intelligence. The plain, clever woman has more magnetism than the pretty, foolish woman. It is quite true that wise men have often been seduced by physical charms alone. Goethe married a doll, and soon wearied of her society. Heine wedded with an illiterate working girl, and bitterly lamented his error of judgment. A pretty woman with an undeveloped mind is far more difficult to manage than a less comely woman, with a reasoning faculty and a knowledge of human nature.

Woman's potentiality remains undeveloped through neglect, through repression, and through scarcity of opportunity. We have so mismanaged women that they have, in vast masses, become curiously automatic, fixed in their ideas and views, and appallingly dull-witted. There is a host of incredibly narrow and silly women in England, an amorphous tribe, with scarcely an intellectual trait, an aspiration, or an ideal. They " suckle fools and chronicle

small beer "; they live on an animal plane, and
eating, sleeping, and decking themselves form
their daily round.   There are whole streets and
suburbs of such women.

It is always more difficult for a woman than
for a man to escape from a bad environment.
Unconventionality costs more to women than to
men, because there are a hundred social laws for
women which men can disregard with impunity.
Originality in men is looked upon with dispas-
sion at least, and is often admired.   In women
originality is almost a crime.   Harriet Mar-
tineau thrusts her manuscripts under her needlework when callers come.   It is " unfeminine "
for a woman to write.   Mary Somerville is
forced to work in secret because science is not a
" womanly " study.   A little girl romps like a
boy.   She is told that little girls must not play
in a natural manner.   These inhibitions could
be multiplied to any extent.   Need we wonder
that girls grow up into mere things of sex,
creatures that have lost almost all the finer human
attributes?   And this is the status, this is the
upbringing, advocated as proper for the mothers
of the race!

Let us briefly review the opinion of modern
thinkers upon woman's capacities in the fields
of politics, social work, and intellectual labour.

Many years ago Burdach observed that women are probably more fitted for political responsibility than men. The same thought was expressed by J. S. Mill. "Among all races and in all parts of the world," writes Havelock Ellis, "women have ruled brilliantly and with perfect control over even the most fierce and turbulent hordes. Among many primitive races also all the diplomatic relations with foreign tribes are in the hands of women, and they have sometimes decided on peace or war. The game of politics seems to develop many feminine qualities in those who play at it, and it may be paying no excessive compliment to women to admit the justice of old Burdach's remarks. Whenever their education has been sufficiently sound and broad to enable them to free themselves from fads and sentimentalities, women probably possess in at least as high a degree as men the power of dealing with the practical questions of politics. Professor G. L. Duprat, in his *Morals*, says: "Woman becomes more and more capable of work and sustained effort. The competition of the sexes in the studio, in teaching, and in all the liberal professions is beginning to be quite appreciable. In particular she brings into her intellectual activity qualities of subtlety, penetration, and vivacity, which, in spite of a

H

generally well-marked mental instability, make
her assistance in the work of civilisation of
increasing value."

M. Lourbet, in *Le Problème des Sexes*, writes,
"The apparent inferiority of woman is acci-
dental, provisional, and external in the indefinite
evolution of humanity, this inferiority having
its principle in the physical minority."

On the assumption that women who desire
emancipation are "masculine," Otto Weininger
—who was anything but a feminist—states:
"Men will have to overcome their dislike for
masculine women, for that is no more than a
mean egoism. If women ever become masculine by becoming logical and ethical, they would
no longer be such good material for man's pro-
jection."

So long as the element described by Nietzsche
as the "abysmal antagonism" exists in the relations of men and women, men will strive to
hinder the intellectual advance of women.
There will be a great struggle in the near future,
in which sex-jealousy and sex-rivalry will rankle
and manifest themselves. In this strife women
will almost lose temporarily many of their graces
and feminine attractions, and stand up as
doughty intellectual Amazons at open war with
men.

Do not imagine, O man, that your long supremacy can endure for ever. You will fare ill in this encounter unless you calmly recognise that the only way to manage the determined militant woman is by arbitration and compromise. You can't manage her with a club. She never was managed with a club. Ask the nearest savage if I am wrong. You have fostered in woman an art of cunning with which no living man can cope in the long-run. Even Mr. Asquith will be vanquished by the wily and indomitable Suffragettes.

CHAPTER VIII.

CAN THERE BE PEACE?

Is the great Sex War interminable? This is a question that concerns the sociologist, the reformer, the politician, and the man in the street. A house divided against itself cannot stand; and a state of society with the sexes at variance, divided in aims and ideals and sundered by misunderstanding, is insecure. The antagonism in love and in family life has now spread into the arena of commerce and industrialism, and into the realms of politics. The " eternal feminine " baffles us. Woman, always a " tormenting joy," as Havelock Ellis has it, is one of the chief problems of the age.

As I write this, we are witnessing a revolt in Spain, which plainly points to the growing power of woman throughout Europe. Spain is one of the least progressive of European countries, and yet Spanish women, in spite of the Oriental rule which has hindered their advance for centuries, are the principal agitators in a rebellion that threatens to upheave the whole legislative system of the nation. The women of Spain have declared that their husbands and sons shall not be sent to the war. It is an uprising of women, and the more remarkable when we realise that thousands of Spanish women cannot read or write. Reflect upon what might be achieved if all the cultured women of a nation united for a political end! No monarch, no parliament, no army could withstand them. Man's protective instinct and his love for woman forbid open physical warfare with her. Hence woman's strength is largely her weakness.

Peace within the home and in the State are imperative. Internecine strife is a cause of insecurity and of reaction in either sphere. To establish peace, or, at least, to lessen animosity, is essential to the future well-being of the community. This can only be achieved by a general rout of all the flagrant misconceptions of the sexes regarding one another. Men must study to understand woman, and how to manage her. Militant women must modify their views upon the injustice, selfishness, and oppressive tendencies of men, qualities that they tend to exaggerate.

When the average man discourses upon woman, he is wont to affirm that Nature intended her to do this, or not to do that, without any previous necessary investigation in physiology. The theory, for example, that women are incapable of intellectual equality with men, by reason of their smaller brains, has now been proved fallacious and worthless. Brain size and brain weight are in proportion to bodily size and weight. It is the opinion of latter-day physiologists that the average brain weight of women is not smaller than that of men, in proportion to body weight. Many men of action have had small brains. Gambetta had a small brain. If it is a question of "brain mass," women are better off than men, for their brains are relatively bigger.

But of what use are our organs if they are neglected and atrophied? The "worse than South Sea isle taboo" that has cramped women's intelligence has induced wasting of the brain potentiality. The stupid usages of costume and the neglect of robust exercises have wasted and deformed the physique of women. Many men suppose that the pinched waists of civilised women are normal and natural! Many men think that it is natural for a woman in health to tire upon slight bodily exertion.

The functional periodicity is often brought forward as a serious handicap upon woman, and cited as a reason why she is likely to fail, or break down recurrently, in a life devoted to business, social affairs, and politics. Disturbances of a physical and mental character undoubtedly occur periodically in women; but many of the disorders are the result of injudicious living, a lack of hygienic knowledge being exceedingly common amongst the sex.

Maternity offers a more serious bar to woman's activities outside of the home. But the puerperal period is not the whole of a woman's life, and many women have small families, or remain childless all their lives.

Man sees woman through a glamour of poetry and romance, and it is well that he does so, for social life is impossible without ideals and illusions. Nor is man's perception all fantasy and the "unsubstantial pageant of a dream." Woman is æsthetically delightful. She has been framed in this wise by Nature, with a very definite purpose. Her long silken hair, whether of gold or sable, is a joy to behold. Her face is often beautiful, and never without its charm for the lover; while her body, with its glorious curves and delicately-textured flesh, imbues a man with a sense of delight, and even of worship, for its superb grace.

Woman's mind and soul are enchanted regions

into which we love to peer and enter. Her
childish innocence calls for our tender affection,
and we learn great lessons from her woman's
native philosophy. She consoles, she heals, and
she inspires man.

But man has to live in the most intimate of
all human relations with this being, whose
charms and whose virtues dazzle and enthral
him. He is bound to know more of woman
than his senses convey, and he cannot always
remain love-dazed and enraptured. His mate
is not always gracious and kind; her daily life
is not always serene through the exercise of her
sweet reasonableness. She is often perverse,
difficult, intractable, spiteful, unmanageable, and
exasperating. "*Souvent femme varie.*"

"Why do women vary in this quick, perplex-
ing manner?" is a question that every husband
asks himself sooner or later. This variability is
not altogether the work of Satan. Much of it
is inevitable, uncontrollable, like the changes of
the moon. Accept this as an axiom, and when
you are distraught by a woman's caprice, unkindness, and ill-temper, remember that you also are
dominated, though in a lesser degree, by functional processes. Remember that a nervous
woman often acts like an insane person when
over-tired or hungry. A hungry woman is an

angry woman. We have all heard the prescription, " Feed the brute." Let us never forget that women are quite as irascible as men when suffering from hunger. Therefore, " Feed the darling."

A lack of control over the temper in women is often associated with a physical cause, which makes control more than normally difficult. It is well to bear this in mind, and to be prepared for outbursts. Bad temper is also a result of blood pressure on the brain; so that anything which lessens that pressure, and draws the blood-flow to other parts of the body, is beneficial. Exercise is essential to the health of most women ; but nervous, excitable women frequently over-exert themselves in walking, cycling, or tennis. On the other hand, a turbulent maniac may be quieted if he can be induced to labour in the fields; and a moderate amount of physical activity is excellent for a neuropathic woman.

It is not always sheer perversity and feminity that cause a woman to blow hot and cold by turn. This must be understood by every lover if he wishes to manage his Jill with a minimum of discord. If a woman is unresponsive, do not persist in your ardour. The mood will change. Bide your time. There are mysterious physiological laws controlling this matter.

In love men and women should cry a truce
to that fatal reticence which characterises the
social intercourse of the two sexes. They
should be frank and open; they should learn
each other's secret and intimate thoughts and
desires.   It is not enough to know that a woman
is a good domestic manager, an amiable friend,
and the possessor of a comely figure.   You are
starting on a very long journey alone with this
companion, and in the first stages you will learn
more of her innermost nature than you can con-
ceive during courtship.   Yet many men—perhaps most—start on their conjugal journey
through life with only the haziest apprehension
of the true, hidden emotions and desires of their
partners.

A community in which the majority of the
educated and forceful women are in conflict with
men is in danger of dissolution.   Woman must
be allowed to develop on her own lines, and
portents show clearly that those lines are diverg-
ing from the old track.   If woman is to be
managed at all, she can only be managed by
acceding to all her reasonable political demands
with a good grace.   Evolution is stronger than
politicians.

Woman has ruled in the past in many parts
of the world, and she may rule again.   Professor

Lester Ward writes of this consummation as certain. For good or ill, women are rapidly winning to a status of social equality. The Matriarchate may follow. And the human male may be doomed to the fate of the male bee and spider. Who can tell?

I remember reading a magazine article by J. T. Nisbet, in which he declared that the nation which heeded the counsels of its women had better put up its shutters at once as a dying concern. What nonsense! Here was a writer of the firmest convictions who had never been to the trouble of reading a few facts of biology and ethnology. Nations have listened, and do still listen, to the counsels of their women. There is not a political pie in Europe without women's fingers in it.

Perfect equality is a fine ideal. We like to picture a partnership in business or in marriage, wherein both partners devise and act as equal agents. Is such absolute unity possible? I fear that it is only a dream of perfection. In the vast majority of human associations there is a head, a leader, a predominant partner. Man has been the head of the two sexes for long ages.

Woman's cry for equality is probably a sub-conscious demand for supremacy. I know that women emphasise the fact that they cannot do without men, and that they only desire an equality of rights. Obviously, women cannot do without men; but it does not follow that they will accept equality with men as the final goal of their striving.

Mary Wollstonecraft was careful to point out that she did not wish women to have power over men, " but over themselves." This has been reiterated by many militant modern women. Indeed, we are often assured that woman, and not man, is the worst enemy of woman. It may be that, in many cases, the woman herself is her own worst enemy, and that her sufferings arise from within herself and are only remotely connected with external circumstances.

The deep introspective tendency of woman often becomes a tyranny to herself. She is morbidly addicted to taking her internal machinery to pieces, and looking at it, until it bewilders or frightens her. These are the women who talk constantly about themselves, their souls, their heart-needs, their pent-up griefs, and their weird longings. They are often deficient in a sense of humour, and therefore very hard to manage. The type has been well studied by Van Eeden, in *The Deeps of Deliverance*.

The failure of the old civilisations of Greece

and Rome was largely due to the wastage of women's powers. Education was the privilege of the courtesan class alone. For centuries women have been educated only to please the opposite sex. The novels and essays of the seventeenth and eighteenth centuries contain fullest proof of this narrowing influence.

" The education of women should be always relative to that of men," wrote Rousseau. " To please, to be useful to us, to make us love and esteem them, to educate us when young and take care of us when grown up, to advise, to console us, to render our lives easy and agreeable : these are the duties of women at all times, and what they should be taught in their infancy."

The setting of woman on an entirely different plane from that occupied by man has always seemed to me a most curious social phenomenon. Women are far more like us in their passions, moral outlook, and aspirations than the bulk of both men and women imagine. That there are specific masculine and feminine traits is undeniable; but the division has been drawn too widely, and many so-called " feminine characteristics " are the products of an unnatural condition.

In our mismanagement of one-half of our population, we have ignorantly determined that woman has but one duty and one function.

What madness!   We do not rear our mares simply to breed colts.   We have also other uses for our horses than as sires.

The way of peace is through the annihilation of the prejudices and preconceptions to which I have frequently referred in these pages.

> " Never shall peace and human nature meet
> Till, free and equal, man and woman greet
> Domestic peace."

If Woman, after her long subjugation, were suddenly freed, and raised to such power as men now possess, we might reasonably anticipate disaster to society.   But there is little fear of such a sex revolution.   The transformation of woman will not be sudden, as from the waving of a fairy wand, but a tedious and painful process in which both sexes will suffer.

May the fates in their mercy still leave us Woman, the essential WOMAN, with at least some traces of those gifts and attractions that we, as sons of Adam, rejoice in!   May Destiny shape her and us in such fashion that we learn to love more and to torment one another less.

THE END.

WALTER WATTS AND CO., LTD., PRINTERS, LEICESTER.

NEW PUBLICATIONS

Issued by

WERNER LAURIE, Clifford's Inn, London.

SPECIAL MESSENGER:
A Novel.

By ROBERT W. CHAMBERS.

Author of "The Fighting Chance," "Cardigan."

Crown 8vo, 6/-.

This novel is one of the most dramatic and romantic which Mr. Chambers has written. It tells thrillingly the life of a girl who volunteered her services as a special messenger in the stressful times of the war between North and South in the States. She is a dashing horsewoman, bold, intrepid, carrying her life in her hands, and is entrusted with work requiring great skill and a greater nerve and aptitude for scouting than a man could possibly undertake. She is often in danger, frequently very near to death, with the blood of her soldier ancestors buoying her up on those occasions when she reveals herself as "but yet a woman."

Mr. Chambers' delineation of such a character is a fine piece of work, powerful and enthralling.

Despite the grimness and ghastliness of the war scenes, the tenderness of the girl stands out through it all as a welcome relief to the tension.

There is, of course, a love element, but this is never maudlin, and studied apart from the fighting, is one of the finest love stories ever written. Clean, wholesome, invigorating. The publisher predicts a big success for this book among all classes of readers.

A WINTER'S COMEDY.

By HALLIWELL SUTCLIFFE.

Author of "Red o' the Feud."

Crown 8vo, 6/-.

Is concerned with the intrusion of Saul Dene, a nouveau riche, into a Yorkshire county set. Saul is unaffectedly rough and he has settled. The mystery of this love, and of the identity of Saul Dene, runs through the book, as does the secret connected with his niece, Phyllis. Phyllis comes to do the honours of the big house, newly purchased, and in every respect she is a contrast to her uncle—she is, in fact, an unmistakable " hark-back " to the type of beauty celebrated through the county as " The Gwynn beauty." Gwynn of Gwynn is their neighbour in the county, but, unable to keep up his family home, he lives in the dower-house, seeing no chance of building up the fortunes of his race again. Phyllis, though brought up in West Kensington by a narrow-minded aunt, comes into this county life—which she has never known—with odd dignity and ease, as if it were familiar to her. She goes for the first time to Gwynn's untenanted house, and everything there, too, is familiar, including the portrait of Gwynn's mother—a portrait for which Phyllis herself might have sat. The county is bewildered by the likeness of this niece of rough Saul Dene's to the Gwynn type—in face, and voice, and manner.

Only Saul and the aunt in West Kensington know the secret, and they keep it jealously until Phyllis has to be told it; and in the telling is unfolded a romance that had set the county in a blaze a generation before. Saul Dene, himself, has his own hidden romance, concerned with Gwynn's mother; and it is for her sake, no less than for Phyllis', that he works quietly and patiently throughout the book to free Gwynn and Phyllis from the tangle which other people are making of their lives, and to restore the ruined fortunes of the Gwynns. Across the comedy there comes a cloud of what threatens to be tragedy, and Halliwell Sutcliffe returns for awhile to the moor atmosphere associated with his work.

THE MARRIAGE OF
HILARY CARDEN.

By STANLEY PORTAL HYATT.
Author of " The Little Brown Brother."

6/-.

First Review :—" Mr. Hyatt has drawn a very powerful picture. He has succeeded brilliantly in creating a dozen or more living persons, and moving them about among scenes which he forcibly

BLACK SHEEP.

By STANLEY PORTAL HYATT.

Author of " The Marriage of Hilary Carden."

6/-.

A vividly-drawn picture of a wandering journalist, who falls in love, and his experiences when introducing the girl to his stodgy mid-Victorian family.

THE UNCOUNTED COST.

By MARY GAUNT.

Author of " The Silent Ones," " Fools Rush In," etc.

6/-.

A story rich in the romance of the sea, and set forth with such artistic charm and deftness of touch that it holds the reader's interest from beginning to end.

MASTER JOHN.

By SHAN F. BULLOCK.

Author of " Robert Thorne—the Story of a London Clerk"

6/-.

The story of an Irish car driver, who narrates wittily all he knows of " Master John," the village doctor's son.

SCARLET KISS.
The Story of a Degenerate Woman.

By GERTIE de S. WENTWORTH-JAMES.

Author of " The Wild Widow."

6/-.

This novel hits off all kinds of feminine artifices and intrigues in a very bright, amusing, merciless and up-to-date manner.

DOWNWARD, a Slice of Life.

By MAUD CHURTON BRABY.

Author of " Modern Marriage, and How to Bear It."

6/-.

THE WINE IN THE CUP.

By ELEANOR WYNDHAM.

Author of "The Lily and the Devil."

6/-.

Cynthia, a magnificent specimen of womanhood is brought up on a lonely island off the Coast of Ireland. When her hump-backed cousin comes along she gladly marries him. The story concerns their marriage, and how they got on together.

THE WICKED WORLD.

By ALICE MAUD MEADOWS.

6/-.

This popular authoress has given in her new novel a trenchant word picture of the life and amusements of the smart set.

THE UNSEEN THING.

By ANTHONY DYLLINGTON.

Author of "The Green Domino."

6/-.

The hero is the victim of an extraordinary physical repulsion to deformity of any kind, which leads him to desert the cousin to whom he is engaged, after having caused the accident by which she has been lamed for life.

GOD'S MAGDALEN.

By OLIVE CHRISTIAN MALVERY.

Author of "The Soul Market."

6/-.

A really big book, dealing poignantly with the life of a slum girl.

RETRIBUTION.

By RANGER GULL.

6/-.

Probably the most exciting and sensational story this author

THE BUTLER'S STORY.
By ARTHUR TRAIN.

6/-.

Peter Ridges, butler in a very new and very rich family, relates in a highly original and entertaining way the various adventures of a social, financial, and sentimental kind that come under his notice.

THE FORBIDDEN THEATRE.
By KEIGHLEY SNOWDEN.
Author of " The Life Class."

6/-.

" ' The Forbidden Theatre,' to put it shortly, is to be put among the few ' best novels ' of the season, and should widen and strengthen its author's position in the regard of discriminating fiction readers."—" Daily Telegraph."

EGYPT (LA MORT DE PHILAE).
By PIERRE LOTI.

Translated by W. P. Baines, and with eight plates in colour from paintings by Augustus O. Lamplough.

Demy, Illustrated, 15/- net.

A wonderfully fascinating book, conveying vivid pictures of the charm of Egypt and the marvels of its antiquity. Loti, as is his wont, endeavours to get at the heart of what he sees, as he steeps himself in the enchantment of moonlit temples erected by the most ancient of civilizations, watches the sun set behind the illimitable wastes of the desert, glides over the darkening waters to the half-submerged island of Philae, " Pearl of Egypt," or listens to the mournful song of the boatmen as he drifts on his dahabieh down the Nile; and gradually a comprehension grows upon him of the reasons that made Egypt the first country to awaken from the torpor of barbarism and to build monuments which are the wonder

MY FRIENDS THE FRENCH.

By ROBERT HARBOROUGH SHERARD.

Author of "The Life of Oscar Wilde."

Very fully Illustrated.   Demy 8vo, 12/6 net.

The great interest shown by the reading public in Mr. Robert Sherard's book of Parisian reminiscences "Twenty Years in Paris," decided the publisher to commission the author to write a further volume on the same subject.   In his volume Mr. Sherard relates more entertaining reminiscences of Paris, and at the same time the book is full of shrewd observations of modern social life in France.   Mr. Sherard's reputation as a keen observer of character, as an amusing *raconteur,* and a graphic artist with the pen should guarantee that the volume is amusing and instructive.   His knowledge of different parts of France, as well as of all classes of French society, is most extensive, and his book contains much valuable information of an original nature.

LOVE INTRIGUES OF ROYAL COURTS.

By THORNTON HALL.

Demy, Illustrated, 12/6 net.

In his latest book Mr. Hall describes many of the secret dramas of Royal Courts, and reveals some of their most remarkable scenes.   In his pages, Catherine the Great plays her role; the pretty madcap, Frances Jennings, coquettes with her lovers; and Christina, Queen of Sweden, dazzles the world by the splendours of her Royal gifts.   The author also describes, among others, King Ludwig, the Chevalier D'Eon playing his dual role, now man, now woman; Sophie Dorothea losing a crown for Königsmarck's love; Countess Castiglione, the mysterious Lady of Versailles; Alexander and Draga in the last tragic scene of their love-

THE ARABIAN NIGHTS.

THEIR BEST KNOWN TALES

Re-written by KATE DOUGLAS WIGGIN.

With many full-page illustrations, title page, cover, and end papers in full colours by MAXFIELD PARRISH.

Cloth gilt, with picture jacket in colours. $9\frac{1}{2}$ by $7\frac{1}{4}$, 10/6 net.

This beautiful new edition of these famous stories is certain to be the favourite Christmas child's book. Miss Wiggin can write for children as no other author can, and in this volume she has re-told the Arabian classic with all her charm of style.

Maxfield Parrish has deservedly made a great name for himself as an illustrator, and his picturing of the book leaves nothing to be desired.

Contents :—I. The History of the Fishermen and the Genie; II. The Young King of the Black Isles; III. The Story of Prince Agib; IV. Sinbad in the Valley of Diamonds; V. Sinbad and the Giant; VI. Aladdin and the Wonderful Lamp; VII. Ali-Baba and the Forty Thieves; VIII. Prince Codadad and His Brothers; IX. Gulnare, Queen of the Sea; X. The City of Brass; XI. The Story of the Talking Bird, the Singing Tree and the Golden Water.

THE GRIZZLY BEAR.

The Narrative of a Hunter—Historical, Scientific and Adventurous.

By WILLIAM H. WRIGHT.

With 24 full-page illustrations from photographs.

Crown 8vo, 7/6 net.

In this book Mr. Wright places on record the facts he has gathered and the deductions he has drawn from some twenty-five years of observation of the grizzly bear. First he tells the story of the grizzly from the time when he was discovered early in the last century down to the author's meeting with him, including the scientific classification of the family. Then he gives the narrative of his personal experiences and adventures with the grizzly, and finally he summarizes his observations of the beast's habits and his opinions of his nature. For years Mr. Wright order to study him. This, then, is a book by a man who is both a hunter and a naturalist. It is a first-hand authoritative book about the most interesting of the wild animals.

CONTENTS.

PART I. Historical.—Autobiographical. Early History—Lewis and Clark. Followers of Lewis and Clark. James Capen Adams. The Scientific Classification of Bears.

PART II. My Experiences and Adventures.—My First Grizzly. Five at a Blow. Grizzly Gourmets. Trailing. A Charging Grizzly. At Close Quarters. My First Trip to the Selkirks. The Selkirks Revisited. The Unexpected. A Spring Gun Avoided. A Photographic Expedition. Flashlighting Grizzlies.

PART III. Character and Habits of the Grizzly.—Description and Distribution. Characteristics and Habits. Food and Feeding. Their Fierceness. Their Vitality. Fact versus Fiction. Conclusion.

THE NIGHTSIDE OF PARIS.

By E. B. d'AUVERGNE.

Author of " Lola Montez."

With 24 full-page drawings specially made for the book by Harry Morley.

Demy, Illustrated, 12/6 net.

A companion volume to the ever-popular " Night Side of London." The author knows the Paris of to-day in its every aspect, and with him we ramble in all directions over the Gay City, now mingling with the fashionable crowd on the Grande Boulevarde, now peeping into Maxim's and the haunts of the *haute voce*, then plunging into the darkest and most dangerous slums, the lair of the *Apache* and the *voyou*. Mr. d'Auvergne makes us free of the Latin Quarter, acts as our pioneer to the heights of Montmartre, and introduces us to the dancing halls of the lower quarters, which are as much the rendezvous of the professional criminal as centres of gaiety. All the way, the author entertains us with his keen and humorous appreciation of Parisian life and character, and incisive comparisons between the two great European capitals.

The illustrations reflect the spirit of the text. Mr. Morley's

GILBERT WHITE AND SELBORNE.

By HENRY C. SHELLEY.

Crown, Illustrated, 6/- net.

Editions of Gilbert White's " Natural History of Selborne " are beyond reckoning. It is always one of the first books added to every series of English classics. It maintains its position as a prime favourite with all classes of readers. Yet, strange beyond belief, the man himself, the faithful curate, the delightful friend, the affectionate uncle, the victim of Cupid, has been woefully neglected. Mr. Shelley has addressed this attractive volume to making good that amazing omission. He paints the man as he was, in all his old-world courtesy and charm, and brings to light many winsome personal traits such as must increase the affection in which he is already held. More than that : The book draws a loving and poetic picture of Selborne, that exquisite Hampshire village which White made famous, and numerous artistic photographs help to bring its picturesque scenes before the reader. There is, besides, a third section to the volume, comprising carefully selected passages from the " Natural History of Selborne," showing the naturalist at his best. Emphatically, then, this is *the* book for all who know the " Natural History," and for all who wish to make its acquaintance in the most fascinating manner.

MY SUMMER IN LONDON.

By JAMES MILNE.

Author of " The Romance of a Pro-Consul,"
" The Epistles of Atkins," etc. With
Illustrations from Special Photographs by
W. J. ROBERTS.

6/- net.

The writer of this book is Literary Editor of the " Daily Chronicle," and Editor of the " Book Monthly." He recently moved from a leisurely house in one of the outer suburbs of London, to a flat in its very centre. Now he writes of the contrast which that means in London life ; of London intimate, London seen from within, by one who previously had only worked in it. Such is the idea of the book, and into this frame-work come many personal memories and stories of the well-known people to

Rotten Row and elsewhere, all suggested by living within sound of Big Ben, and it is content to be just good reading, just interesting. As a summer picture of London the book gains greatly from the photographs, which show two things: what beautiful views London has, and how beautifully an artist in photography can present those views.

WHERE THE FISHERS GO.
The Story of Labrador.
By REV. P. W. BROWNE.
(Member Historical Society, Nova Scotia.)

Crown 8vo, with nearly 200 illustrations, 6/- net.

This is one of the few authentic accounts of the Great Peninsula ever published, and no such comprehensive description of Labrador has yet appeared. It makes a unique and interesting volume, by an author whose ancestry were pioneers of the Northland. The numerous illustrations and maps form a helpful supplement to the text.

SPIRIT AND MATTER BEFORE THE BAR OF MODERN SCIENCE.
By Dr. I. HEYSINGER.

Demy, 15/- net.

This book is the first to bring together all the most recent demonstrations of modern science, recent psychology, and comparative religions, bearing upon the great conflict between Materialism and Transcendentalism, which is now substantially concluded.

The book is interesting and extremely readable, as a mere book; it reads like a novel but is as solid as Newton's Principia. The Table of Contents cites the list of authorities for each chapter, and they are numbered by hundreds; and in Part IV. will be found many personal experiments, mostly unpublished.

The student of Religion, and its clergymen and teachers, those interested in Psychology and Philosophy, those seeking to be abreast of modern science, and the intelligent public among whom, throughout the world, these questions are now awaking so great an interest, cannot forbear to read this clearly written presentation of the whole case, supported by a mass of evidence which cannot be controverted while human reason and the methods of science

PSYCHICAL SCIENCE and CHRISTIANITY.

By E. KATHARINE BATES.

Author of "Seen and Unseen," "Do the Dead Depart?"

Crown 8vo, 6s.

This book is not written from the point of view of an "expert," discoursing upon the Higher Criticism or the so-called New Theology.

It is written primarily for that large and increasing class of intelligent readers, who may not air their opinions in the Hibbert Journal or other organs of advanced Theological Thought, but who have, nevertheless, given many hours of anxious reflection to the present imminent and critical times of readjustment and reconstruction. The old garments of hard and fast Theological creeds are outgrown, having served their necessary purpose in the past, Modern discoveries and modern freedom of thought prove this beyond question.

PRACTICAL HYPNOTISM.
Theories and Experiments.

Compiled and Edited

By COMTE C. de SAINT-GERMAIN.

From the works of Braid, Charcot, Luys, Liébault, Wetterstrand Bernheim, Moll, De Courmelles, Etc.

Crown 8vo, 6/- net.

The Dawn of Hypnotism. From Mesmer to Braid. Prof. Charcot and his School. Mental Theory advocated at Nancy. The Charité Hospital Experiments. Progress of the Study Outside of France. The Four Different Stages of Hypnotic Sleep. The Intermediate Stage or Fascination State. The Theory of Hypnotism. Who can Hypnotise. Who is Hypnotisable. How to Induce the Hypnotic State. How to Awaken Subjects from the

MARY BAKER EDDY—HER LIFE, HER WORK.

By WILFRID SOAMES.

Crown 8vo, 3/6 **net.**

The author of this book is not a Christian Scientist, but has always taken a strong and sympathetic interest in Mrs. Eddy and her work.

He endeavours to set forth for the man in the street a plain statement of the life, work, and aims of the leader of the Christian Scientists for the benefit of the ordinary person who desires to know more of this vast and still rapidly-growing movement.

NEW IDEALS IN HEALING The Emmanuel Movement).

By RAY STANNARD BAKER.

12 Full-page Illustrations.

Fscp. 8vo, 2/6 net.

This is the first book on the "Emmanuel Movement" and allied activities to be written by an impartial observer and a trained writer on public affairs who has at his command a clear and interesting style.

He not only describes the "Emmanuel Movement," but reveals it as one manifestation of the great spiritual unrest pervading the nation.

Mr. Baker explains the almost miraculous cures by such clergymen as Dr. Worcester. He then goes further to show how doctors are using the control of mind over body to effect similar cures. Altogether it is a live book on a tremendously live subject.

THE QUINTESSENCE OF NIETZSCHE.

By J. M. KENNEDY.

Crown, Illustrated, 6/- net.

This book is interesting not only as giving the first full account in English of Nietzsche's complete works, including the recently-published posthumous writings and fragments, but also and to British institutions in general. The publication of the fragmentary works and letters has thrown new light on Nietzsche's opinions concerning love, woman, and marriage, all of which are referred to or cited in the course of the work. Quotations are given from all Nietzsche's writings, no work of the philosopher being left unmentioned. For the chapters dealing with Nietzsche's life, studies, travels, etc., Mr. Kennedy quotes the newly-issued autobiography, *Ecce Homo*. The volume is provided with a short bibliography, and a full index.

EGOISTS. A Book of Supermen.
By JAMES HUNEKER.

Author of " Iconoclasts," " Melomaniacs."

With portrait of Stendhal: Unpublished Letters of Flaubert; and Original Proof Page of Madame Bovary.

Contents :—Henri Beyle-Stendhal. The Baudelaire Legend. The Real Flaubert. Anatole France. Joris-Karl Huysmans. Maurice Barres. Phases of Nietzsche. Mystics: Ernest Hello, William Blake, Francis Poictevin, The Road to Damascus, Ibsen. Max Stirner.

Mr. Huneker discusses in an illuminating and striking manner such men as Stendhal, whose cult, recently revived on the Continent, is steadily growing; Anatole France, blithe pagan and delicious ironist; Max Stirner, and other poets, philosophers and prose writers whose writings embody the individualistic idea as opposed to altruistic and socialistic sentiment. The knowledge, vigor and brilliancy of Mr. Huneker's writings bring these extraordinary and important men vividly before the public that as yet knows little about most of them.

MODERN WOMAN AND HOW TO MANAGE HER.
By WALTER M. GALLICHAN.

Crown 8vo, 3/6 net.

Chapter I.—An Agelong Conflict.—The Sexes at Variance—Why Women Torture their Lovers—Are Women Gentle? Chapter II.—The Warfare To-Day.—The Eternal Misunderstanding between the Sexes. Women's Emotionality and its Spurious

Chapter III.—The Duel in Love.—Falling in Love—Its Effect upon Men—Its Influence upon Women—The Differences between the Love of Men and Women—Why Women Like Long Engagements. Chapter IV.—The War in Wedlock.—Ideal Marriage—Marriage as it often is—Why Conjugality is frequently a State of Warfare—Is the Free Union a Greater Success than Marriage? Chapter V.—The Feud in the Family.—The Revolt of the Daughters—The British Father—The British Matron—The Advanced Daughter—The Escape from Home-Life—Women in Clubs. Chapter VI.—The Strife in Breadwinning.—Women in the Professions and Trades—Is Woman fit to Work—The "Social Evil." Chapter VII.—The Battle in Politics.—The Dreaded Rule of Women—The Struggle for Freedom—The Woman's Suffrage—Crusade and its Lessons. Chapter VIII.—Can there be Peace?—A Plea for the Freer Association of the Sexes—Supremacy or Equality?

STORIES FROM THE OPERAS
(Third Series).
By GLADYS DAVIDSON.

Crown 8vo, Illustrated, 3/6 net.

Owing to the kind reception accorded to Miss Gladys Davidson's first and second series of "Stories From the Operas," she has been encouraged to prepare a third supplementary volume of these charming tales. The object of the writer has been to present all the incidents of each opera dealt with in the clear readable form of a short story, and apart from the special appeal they make to the opera-goer, the three volumes provide a unique collection of dramatic tales of absorbing interest to the general reader, which all lovers of good stories should certainly add to their libraries.

CHATS ON ELECTRICITY.
By FRANK BROADBENT, M.I.E.E.

Crown 8vo, fully illustrated, 3/6 net.

There are a large number of books on electricity dealing with the matter from the technical side, and quite a considerable number dealing with it from the popular point of view. There appears, however, to be a need for something which, whilst not technical, is of such a character as to give to the general non-technical reader has been so rapid of recent years that it has not been possible for the lay mind to follow them merely from the ordinary newspaper descriptions, and this little work is intended to give him such information as shall permit him to obtain an intelligent grasp of electrical principles, such as will enable him to follow the course of events.

CHATS ON ASTRONOMY.

By H. P. HOLLIS.

Of the Royal Observatory, Greenwich.
President of the British Astronomical Association.

Crown 8vo, fully illustrated, 3/6 net.

This book answers many questions that a child, or even the average grown-up educated person asks about the astronomical facts that we are all meeting in everyday life. Why does the sun set at different times during the year? Why does it change its setting point? Why do we see Orion's belt only in the winter months? Why do we see the Great Bear always? Is Venus the evening star at the same dates in each year? How often is she bright? Why does the moon change its shape? What are shooting stars? Why is Greenwich time better than other kinds? How does a sailor know where he is when he is at sea? How do we know how large the earth is? How many stars are there? How does an astronomer work? Are there people in Mars? Etc., etc.

These are a few of the questions answered in simple language by one of the greatest experts of the day.

The book contains many interesting and informing illustrations.

(IN THE CATHEDRAL SERIES).

OLD ENGLISH TOWNS.

By WILLIAM ANDREWS.

Author of " Bygone England," etc.

Crown 8vo, fully illustrated, 6/- net.

In this charming volume are included descriptive and historical accounts of the more important of our old English towns. Sketches of the chief buildings of past ages, remarkable episodes, curious old laws regulating the religious and social life of bygone ages are noticed in scholarly style. It is shown how cities have risen

care of religious houses, while some have advanced under t'
patronage of kings. Old customs linked with the daily life
the people receive consideration. Sports and pastimes which h?
made the inhabitants famous are not forgotten. This is a volu
for the general reader, and also the student who delights in
picturesque past.

(IN THE CATHEDRAL SERIES).

THE CATHEDRALS AND CHURCHES OF BELGIUM.

By T. FRANCIS BUMPUS.

With many Illustrations. Crown 8vo, 6/- ne'

This is probably the most interesting of the Cathedral serie
and the talented author has treated the subject in a most delightfu
and fascinating manner.

To the student of Gothic architecture, the author's descriptio'
of the Romanesque nave and apsidal transepts, and the point
choir of Tournai Cathedral will afford much delight; while tho'
whose predilections are for homogeneity of design will be gratifie
by his enthusiastic accounts of the grand proportions and spacio'
majesty not only of such widely visited churches as those
Antwerp, Bruges, Brussels, Ghent, Liége, Louvain, and Malin'
but of Aerschot, Alost, Lierre, Mons, Ou Leualde, Tongres, a.
Ypres.

THE LIFE OF GEORGE MORLAND.

By GEORGE DAWE, R.A.

With an Introduction and Notes by J. J.
FOSTER, F.S.A. Sumptuously illustrated by
over 50 Plates reproduced by the finest
method of Photogravure. A New Edition
with hand-coloured Frontispiece.

3/3/0 net.

Morland loved nature and went direct to it for his inspiration,
his works are redolent of the fields, of the woods and of the
shore; and he always speaks to us with a genuine native born

CPSIA information can be obtained at www.ICGtesting.com
Printed in the USA
LVOW09s1609310813

350428LV00013B/403/P